BEAUTIFUL TOMBS

MAGDA KING

Beautiful Tombs
Magda King
Copyright © 2019
0803 855 0570

Written in 2004
First Published as Ebook in 2012
Published on Amazon in 2013

Published by
The House of Bezaleel
"The BeautyParlour"
Carmel
Ibadan, Nigeria
E-mail:beautyparlour05@yahoo.com

http://www.amazon.com/kemi-jorge-oyewusi/e/BOOGE6DPD8

ISBN: 978-1493724178

Unless otherwise stated, all Scripture quotations are from the The Amplified Bible, © Copyright 1995 by The Zondervan Corporation.

DEDICATION

To the greatest love of my life. My best friend, my heartbeat, my soul-mate, the very reason I am. You pardon my many faults and continuously clean me up, all because you love me - My God, my King, my Redeemer - JESUS!

To everyone born of God who desires to BECOME.

ACKNOWLEDGMENT

Deep true love, oneness, total conscious commitment, spirit
loaded counsel, full support with fatherly dedication and
brotherly devotion, all encourage me daily and give me
wings to fly to fulfil all that I have
been called to. Jehovah bless and reward you my Priest:
TEMINIKANSOSO

Profound gratitude and love to the COMPETENT
bricklayers of the foundation:
Francis Adekunle Ogunyemi
Victor Olasunkanmi Adeyemi
Willy Bunting
Benson Idahosa
Sam Tukura
Emmanuel Nuhu Kure

Expressions of deep divine truths from priceless
mentorship and invaluable wholesome fellowship,
I appreciate you:
Ayodeji Olorunda

Wholehearted passionate love to my precious Jewels:
Mokunfayo
Pipeniseoluwa
Tadeniawo
Aseirorun

CONTENT

INTRODUCTION

W hen they did not believe it was important to have a true knowledge of God, God gave them up and allowed them to wallow in their own worthless thinking. And so they were left to do the things they were not supposed to do.

These people are filled with every known kind of sin and evil. They are filled with lies, murder, fornication, gossip, jealousy, fighting, adultery, fraud and so on. These people really hate God. They are conceited, full of themselves and very rude. They are always inventing new ways of doing evil.

These people know God's law and they know that the way they live is wrong, that people who live like this should die. But regardless of this, they continue in their ways and encourage and support those who do these things. (Paraphrased from Romans 1:28-32, ETRV.)

They preach one message, but they actually practice another. They seek and demand the praise and respect of men. They parade their religion and seek chief places and positions in the body of believers.

They glory in personal attention. They call attention to themselves not to God. They glory in titles, big titles. They rob men of truth and life and they themselves reject truth and life.

They are zealous to win people to their assemblies but not to God. They profess to be the authority on spiritual matters but they themselves are blind and cannot discern truth and true practical Christianity.

They publish and spread their own interpretation of the gospel especially the parts that are most beneficial to them. They prefer to lay emphasis on minor details and omit the real issues that are important to right living.

They stress and emphasize outward appearances and outward presentation but live in moral depravity and decadence. They exhibit outward holiness and outward righteousness but ignore inner holiness that flows from deep within. They flaunt external prosperity and physical beauty, but inside they are ugly and dead, full of decomposition and all forms of putrification.

> 25. *Woe to you, scribes and Pharisees, pretenders (hypocrites)! For you clean the outside of the cup and of the plate, but within they are full of extortion (prey, spoil, plunder) and grasping self-indulgence.*
> 26. *You blind Pharisee! First clean the inside of the cup and of the plate, so that the outside may be clean also.*
> 27. *Woe to you, scribes and Pharisees, pretenders (hypocrites)! For you are like tombs that have been whitewashed, which look beautiful on the outside but inside are*

full of dead men's bones and everything impure.

28. *Just so, you also outwardly seem to people to be just and upright but inside you are full of pretense and lawlessness and iniquity.*

33. *You serpents! You spawn of vipers! How can you escape the penalty to be suffered in hell (Gehenna)?*

Matthew 23: 25-28, 33

Chapter One

THE DECORATED GRAVE

The crowd tonight was mammoth. It was almost three times what it was yesterday. The auditorium was filled beyond its capacity and bursting at its seams. People overflowed out to the lawn and onto the parking lot.

It was unimaginable. The posters had gone out quite late and no one in the office had thought it was possible to get people out here at such short notice. In fact, Muriel had all but asked for a cancellation. Her thinking was that it was only going to be a waste of time and resources.

Anyway, here they were and the crowd was keeping all the staff jumping and running. Things had to be kept on an even keel.

"Where on earth could they get an additional twenty-five thousand seats at this time?" They needed more speakers and also two more big screens, and it was almost 7pm. The eight hundred-strong choir was screeching at the top of their voices despite the public address systems and still they could hardly be heard. It was time for the choir to take a break.

Muriel knew she needed some serious help, and fast too. This was 4.35pm. The Lord Apostle's caravans were just driving into the Arena and that meant the Apostle himself was not too far behind. He always arrived three hours after his caravans. Things must be sorted out before he gets there or else someone's head was going to roll. There were no two guesses as to who that someone would be.

The Arena had been originally designed as a camping ground. It had the capacity to accommodate crowds, but tonight the arena choked with the multitudinous crowd that had gathered for the meeting.

"O God! Please let Andrey be in Queenstown, I need her now more than ever," Muriel prayed silently. Andrey, Muriel's sister, played in a big jazz band and she was also the janitor at the 35,000-sitter Coleman Louis Auditorium here in Queenstown. So, seeing her would settle the seats, the screens and the speakers all in one go.

Two hours and thirty minutes later Muriel felt a lot better. She and her team were going to get top marks for a job well done. The crowd had settled down on the seats out on the lawn and parking area. The screens were serving them well. The choir looked more relaxed as they sang. The rented speakers were an answer to prayer.

The arena grounds was sitting on 5hectares of land, comprising a 80,000-sitter auditorium with a huge parking lot, a large shopping mall, an amusement park, a zoo, baths, and a large assortment of facilities. It was a grand place to be.

Tonight everyone on the arena grounds had gathered for the meeting.

Everything was in place. The Lord Apostle's books were out on the bookstands. All the 1,200 titles and there were at least 2,000 copies of each book. It would be a roaring sale.

At 7.25 pm, right on the dot of time, the Lord Apostle, Nankalan Aleo Gamonifini's convoy drove into the arena. As his retinue of limousines rolled slowly by, one could hear the speakers from each vehicle blaring in unison the song, "You are glorious, so glorious is your name." The man sure knew how to make an entrance.

The convoy continued to the north side of the arena away from the auditorium situated on the south side. Quick as lightning, the bodyguards leaped out of the cars and surrounded the Lord Apostle's metallic gold, bulletproof, stretch limousine as it rolled to a stop outside his parked private caravan. Engine still running, the right side back window of the limousine cracked open, the Lord Apostle crooked his fore finger and beckoned to Muriel who was already standing by… she rushed forward.

"How strong is our crowd tonight?" Nankalan's big, strong voice growled.

"Well, my Lord, we must have at least a triple of what was here yesterday," Muriel answered.

"How many television networks are stationed here?" he asked again.

"Five my Lord," Muriel answered.

"I hope the additional security is in place? I will not have my vehicles looted or vandalized by hoodlums!" Nankalan spat out.

"It's all well taken care of my Lord," Muriel stated.

"Good, good, and is all well?"

"All is well my Lord," answered Muriel, Senior Personal Assistant to the Lord Apostle and Coordinating Director of the Righteous Shepherd Ministries Worldwide.

The window went back up and immediately two guards moved swiftly, one to the car door and the other to the caravan door. In unison, the guards threw open the doors and Nankalan stepped out from his limousine and walked briskly into the caravan.

Muriel went in and shut the door after them. The guards quickly stationed themselves round the caravan. Already news had gone through the arena that the Lord Apostle's convoy had been sighted driving in. He needed all the security he could get now. Actually, ever since the mobile kitchen and mobile staff quarters arrived the night before, the whole arena had been agog with extreme excitement.

Nankalan went straight to his marble study desk to make last minute checks on his sermon notes. Not that he needed to, he could preach tonight's sermon without opening to his notes or even to the Bible. He had everything in his head. Muriel poured him some cool water in his special pure gold goblet. It had diamond and sapphire studs worked into it. It had been specially hand crafted for him from Valencia. The

Lord Apostle always needed a glass of water before going to the pulpit. He said it helped clear his head and cleanse his spirit.

"My dear Muriel, you are so good to me… is everything ready for me now and after?" Nankalan turned to Muriel asking;

"Yes most holy one," Muriel bowed her head; "I have made sure everything is just as you would want it," she answered.

"The Lord bless you especially my dear," Nankalan said as he turned from his desk and went into the opulent bedroom space where his clothes had been neatly laid out for him and his lizard skin shoes were gleaming by his shoe stand.

"Please leave me now, I need to get some rest before I am ready. Hold all calls and tell them I am in a special prayer session. I will be out in twenty minutes," he said.

Muriel hurried out of the caravan. She told the guards to stand by for The lord Apostle in twenty minutes. He always kept to time. "Thank God he appeared to be in a good mood tonight," Muriel thought to herself. When he was not on the pulpit, "his most holy" had the temper of a "hippo with a hernia." His temper was fierce.

She walked briskly to the auditorium. She had to inform the choir director; the moment the Lord Apostle steps on the threshold, his favourite song must begin.

The crowd was expectant. She knew tonight would be one of those nights. She could feel it already. The Lord Apostle would be pleased.

In exactly twenty-five minutes, 'His Most holy', The Lord Apostle - Nankalan Aleo Dominic Gamonifini - The Presiding Archbishop of The Righteous Shepherd Ministries Worldwide, The Patriarch of The Conquerors Assembly Inc., with his retinue of bodyguards stepped unto the expansive lawn area of the auditorium and the crowd went wild.

He walked slowly through the crowd with his arms held up in the air, and the bodyguards had a whale of a time keeping the crowd at bay. His fingers sparkled with heavy apostle rings and his apostolic robe flowed majestically after him. People struggled to touch him from all sides. Some even threw themselves at his feet; others just screamed, "Nankalan! Nankalan! Blessed servant of the living God!" It was an uproar.

Dropping his guards as he got to the entrance, Nankalan stepped into the 80,000-sitter auditorium and a loud chorus of "All hail King Jesus, All hail Emmanuel!" rent the air.
He headed straight to the pulpit. "Glory be to God on High!" Nankalan bellowed from His wireless microphone. "The Lord is going to richly bless someone tonight!" The crowd went berserk.

"Yes! It was going to be one of those nights," Muriel mused to herself as she walked out of the auditorium. She could see the anointing was strong on The Lord Apostle tonight. That meant 'miracles, 'signs' and 'wonders'. She had to check on the ushers and make sure they had enough designer blankets to keep the slain in the spirit decently covered. "Oh! It promises to be a very busy meeting."

By 10.45pm, Muriel's feet were aching terribly, her head was spinning, but all that was irrelevant now. She had just made all the necessary arrangements to make sure the armoured truck conveying the nights offering was safely out of the arena and at the bank. The Lord Apostle did not trifle with his money. And now she just got the signal on her walkie-talkie from the boys on the altar, His Most holy, would be leaving the pulpit in the next 25 minutes. Everything had to be ready at the caravan.

She rushed out of the arena towards her jeep, which she had tucked neatly behind the wall outside the south gate. About five minutes later, breathing heavily, she tapped on the tinted window. The back seat door opened and a very pretty, very young girl carrying a small duffle bag stepped out. "Quick," Muriel said grabbling her hand, "we must hurry, the meeting is about winding up; you must be ready before he gets to the caravan."

They walked hurriedly, going round the back of the arena to get to the caravan. A much longer route but more secluded. Muriel asked the girl to wait while she distracted the guards so she could sneak her into the caravan with the minimum attention.

Once in, Muriel quickly inspected the laid out dinner table and the rooms, making sure the lights and music were just right. Nothing but the best here. The wine was at room temperature. The movie was playing with the audio cut off, bodies wriggling silently in wild ecstasy. The Lord Apostle would be here any minute from now and everything had to be picture perfect.

Muriel turned to the girl.

"I hope you have everything you need? If you need oils, towels, gels, syrups, toys, anything; you can check in the drawer beside the bed. Please make sure you are undressed, washed and properly shaved before he gets here. He cannot stand filth of any kind. He will be exhausted and he will need the massage first. After then you can use your extensive expertise to unwind and pleasure him. When he is through with you, I will come to take you back to the jeep. Please do not ask him for anything. I have made all necessary arrangements for you. Need I remind you again that you are highly favoured and privileged to partake of His holiness' "anointing." With this, Muriel turned on her heels and walked out of the caravan.

Once outside, she could hear the choir singing "Give and it shall be multiplied to you a hundred fold." It was special offering time. The meeting was winding to a close at last. It sure had been a great meeting.

> *In the last days...people will love pleasure ...*
> *they will not love God. These people will*
> *continue to act like they serve God. But the way*
> *they live shows that they don't really serve God...*
> *stay away from these people*
>
> 2 Timothy 3:4 & 5 (ETRV)

Chapter Two

THE STRENGTH OF THE FLESH

The carnal nature, or the flesh, is the natural state of man. Every man is flesh. The nature of man uninfluenced, untouched by God is the carnal nature.

The carnal nature operates in the realm of the physical. Man is a tripartite being; he is a spirit with a soul and a body. A carnal man is a man under the rule of the soul and the body. A carnal man is a man who is ruled by his flesh. A carnal man is an 'ordinary man,' 'a mere man'.

A carnal man is that Christian man who bases all his reactions on his senses. A carnal man makes all his decisions based on the things he sees, hears, feels, tastes, and touches. This kind of person lives solely by things physical. The carnal man's life revolves around things that are self-gratifying.

There are three laws that govern the carnal nature. They are classified as:

- THE LUST OF THE FLESH
- THE LUST OF THE EYES

- THE PRIDE OF LIFE

The Lust of the Flesh - This is the ardent desire for the things that will please and satisfy our bodies. We disregard what will please or displease God. We insist on satisfying our fleshly desires. We do have legitimate physical needs, however, if we displease God to please and pleasure ourselves then we are walking after the flesh.

We embrace lust when we sport with titbits of sensual pleasure and fool ourselves that by not going all the way into full sexual sin, we are still on the right track. When we do go all the way to satisfy our carnal desires, we have the excuse that we are weak spiritually and we cannot help ourselves, so God understands. At other times, we ignore the consequences and say God is merciful, so we can sin and confess our sins, He will forgive us. At every point in time when we engage lust, we have a plausible excuse, reason, argument or even an already made up pardon in our minds.

The Lust of the Eyes - We want and desire all the things we see. We want all that delights our eyes. We see things, and we covet and desire them. We go all out to acquire what we desire, disregarding if it is right for us in God's eyes or not. We see, we want, we acquire. We believe we must have anything and everything that is pleasing to our eyes, especially if we can. We are consumed by our desires for things.

The Pride of Life - We pursue knowledge, wisdom and develop ourselves so that we can flaunt our expertise. We take immense pride in our achievements and possessions. Our hearts are lifted in pride because of our acquisitions and positions. We glory in our attributes and abilities forgetting that no man receives anything of himself. Position, power and status is key.

> *John answered, A man can receive nothing [he can claim nothing, he can take unto himself nothing] except as it has been granted to him from heaven. [A man must be content to receive the gift which is given him from heaven; there is no other source.]*
>
> John 3:27

We are therefore motivated to pursue things that will give us credit and value in the eyes of the world. We want people to applaud us all the time, so we strive to achieve and acquire for the applause.

A man ruled by these three laws is a man who lives a life that is antagonistic to God, to progress, to joy, to fulfillment and to life. He is an 'ordinary man' who lives to pleasure himself and therefore cannot possibly pleasure God.

> 6. *Now the mind of the flesh [which is sense and reason without the Holy Spirit] is death*

[death that comprises all the miseries arising from sin, both here and hereafter]. But the mind of the [Holy] Spirit is life and [Soul] peace [both now and forever].

7. *[That is] because the mind of the flesh [with its carnal thoughts and purposes] is hostile to God, for it does not submit itself to God's law; indeed it cannot.*

8. *So then those who are living the life of the flesh [catering to the appetites and impulses of their carnal nature] cannot please or satisfy God, or be acceptable to Him.*

Romans 8:6-8

A believer who lives by these three laws is a carnal believer, a carnal Christian. He is dominated by the desire to nourish and satisfy himself. He is consumed by his needs and his wants. He is controlled and motivated by self.

A carnal Christian's life is controlled by his senses, not by the Word of God. He lives according to the things that appeal to him. He does not live according to what God says or wants. This kind of Christian lives by the standards set by the world not by God.

The spiritual leaders of the day in Jesus' time were such believers. Jesus admonished the people concerning them.

2.   *The scribes and Pharisees sit on Moses' seat [of authority]*

3.   *So observe and practice all they tell you; but do not do what they do, for they preach, but do not practice.*

Matthew 23:2-3 (Emphasis Added)

The Word of God in the mouths of such leaders should be obeyed, but their lifestyles must never be copied or emulated.

For they concentrate on their reputations with the people, that is, the way people see them and what the people think about them. They prefer to appear before men as righteous, pious and holy. They focus on outward appearances so they can receive acclaim of men but at the same time, they indulge in their own selfish desires and self-centered past times.

Chapter Three

THE SMOGAD

Justina Philips had just returned from her trip to the South of France. She had had the time of her life.

Justina had wined and dined at the finest restaurants. (It is true that the French know their wine) She had found out that red wine was best taken at room temperature and with beef dishes, while white wine was designed to be taken with fish and different mouth-watering sauces; it was simply divine. She had learned to eat sushi and she had fallen head over heels in love with baguettes and different hot rolls, especially spicy garlic bread.

Her favourite times had been spent in designer shops where she had shopped till she thought she would drop.

Justina felt like a million dollars and she definitely looked it too. All the women would "eat their hearts out" tonight just by looking at her. She took the keys to her Jaguar, "time to go and take them by storm, God is sure an irresistible God."

***

Francine Porter could not just fathom why in the clear blue sky she had decided to wear the green frock again. The fact that it was the only thing in her wardrobe that looked anything like a dinner dress notwithstanding, she should have remembered that this was the fourth time she was wearing it to the SMOGAD in the past two years.

She only hoped that, that "pocked-face" girl was not coming tonight. Francine would just have a seizure right there on the dinner floor. 'Pock face' always had a way of making Francine feel she was dressed in rags.

Anyway, she knows as soon as God answers her prayers and Gregory gets that new job, she would be able to overhaul her wardrobe. "Won't that be something?" At last she would be able to go out of her house without feeling like everyone was looking at her like "something that the cat had just dragged in." Oh well! Nothing to do for now except to make sure tonight she steered clear of all those "mean-mouthed" girls.

***

Apate Doregos could not keep from smiling to herself. It just tickles her to no end anytime she remembers the look on Donny's face when she told him "No, but thank you all the same." Why in God's good name he thought she would agree to something so preposterous she could never comprehend.

She had a lot mapped out on her activity calendar journal for next month. Most of what she had to do would take money. So why on earth would she take an advance on her salary to buy herself a new dinner dress! "Buy a new dress?" What a laugh!

She picked up her 'new' dinner dress she had just made from her mother's old mauve coat, the wonderfully soft shiny green suede rug she had dug up from the trunk in her storage cupboard and some emerald glass buttons she had picked up from the flea market; the dress looked exquisite - to her anyway.

Apate was not going to get herself into a tiffy over a dinner party. Besides, she remembered the story about Moses and his radiant face. She could not believe that anyone remembered what clothes it was Moses was wearing all the time his face had the glow. She was sure his face outshone his garments.

Apate laughed out loud to herself. She knew the joy of the presence of God on the inside of her would radiate all over her tonight. She had scrubbed and cleaned herself up thoroughly. She felt good. She made a mental note to herself, she must get home on time tonight, so much to do in the morning, she needs a good night's rest.

Apate slipped on her exquisite dinner dress and her well-polished black mules. She checked her hair and face, picked up her purse and gave her mirror a 1000-watt smile. She believed she looked divine, she felt it. Apate was ready for the quarterly 'SMOGAD' - St Mary's Old Girls Association Dinner. It would be a very interesting night, she was sure.

Chapter Four

THE OUTSIDE OF THE CUP
AND DISH

M an is a spirit, he has a soul and he lives in a body. So, there is an inward man and an outward man. The outward man is the body or physical state of man. The inward man is the spirit and the soul, this is the inner state of man. This inward or inner man is the real man.

> *"...but though our outward man perish, yet the inward man is renewed day by day."*
> 2 Corinthians 4:16 KJV

The outward or outer life reflects a person's standing with the outside world. The outer life is the lifestyle that is open and obvious to our physical observers, this is the life we present to the viewing world. The outward or outer life is the outward image.

An outward person is a person who places a high premium on how people see him and what people think about him. When we are outward people, this suggests that what people think about us is usually most important to us. We are much concerned about how the world views us. We want the world to note our successes and triumphs. We want to show off our knowledge (the depth, length and breath of it). We have a need to advertise our revelations. We crave the world's applause for our achievements. We desire admiration for our accomplishments. We judge and appraise ourselves by what the world thinks about us.

The world measures quality of life with material standards of living. This places a lot of emphasis on physical and outward appearances.

We are outward Christians, when we believe that what we are on the outside is what reflects the size, the power and the capabilities of our God, or and that our physical and material achievements reflect the kind of standing we have with God. Thus, we need for people to see our lifestyles, our achievements and applaud us and our privileged position. We want the world to acknowledge us, we want people to commend our accomplishments.

All this builds a great thirst and hunger in us for power. Power, pomp and pageantry. The power to build - build structures, build empires, epitaphs and monuments to ourselves. Ostentatious display of wealth and glory.

We do ministry, we organize crusades and revivals, and target mammoth crowds; the focus is not on doing the will of God, the focus is on self. Our passion for souls is to measure success with success - to compare progress with progress.

We seek to outnumber one another. We must have a larger following, a bigger congregation. The maxim is, "The bigger the congregation, the more successful the ministry, the more acclaim the man at the helm receives and the more money comes in."

We are zealous not for God but for ourselves. We talk big and dress even bigger. We play to the people. We are always on centre stage. The world is our theatre. We cannot afford for the world not to see us in affluence and in authority. It matters what the people think and say about us. Image is everything.

King Saul could not bear for the people to think he was not in control, so he defied the law and order of God concerning temple worship. He intruded into the priest's office to save his image. He was a man whose soul was completely taken by the world's standards.

> *Saul waited seven days, according to the set time Samuel had appointed. But Samuel had not come to Gilgal, and the people were scattering from Saul.*
>
> 1 Samuel 13:8

In 1 Samuel 15:21, King Saul disobeyed the direct instructions of God. He had been told not to spare any living thing in the Israelites attack of the Amalekites, yet he did. He gave the excuse that the people took the spoils. God pronounced upon Saul his rejection of him as king.

28. *And Samuel said to him, The Lord has torn the kingdom of Israel from you this day and has given it to a neighbor of yours who is better than you.*

29. *And also the Strength of Israel will not lie or repent; for He is not man, that He should repent.*

30. *Saul said, I have sinned; yet honour me now, I pray you, before the elders of my people and before Israel, and return with me, that I may worship the Lord your God.*

1 Samuel 15:28-30

Here we see that Saul was clearly an outward man. After God had expressly declared his absolute rejection of Saul as king in Israel, the uppermost thing on Saul's mind at that time remained his honour in the eyes of the people - his image.

His destiny was ruined. His life shattered. His place had just been taken from him. The God of Israel had just rejected him and torn the throne of Israel out of his hands. Disgrace, shame, dishonour was covering his face, yet, all that was uppermost on Saul's mind at that time was what the people would think of him.

He urged Samuel the prophet to go with him through the outward motions of worship, so as to satisfy the people and make them believe that all was right. The most important thing to him was that his honour in the eyes of the people be preserved, even though in the eyes of God he was devoid and empty of all honour. It was important to him that the people believe that he was still in control.

Outward Christianity is pitiful, it is dishonour. It is spiritual death, and ultimately physical death, as it happened in the case of King Saul of Israel.

> *But the spirit of the Lord departed from Saul, and an evil spirit from the Lord tormented and troubled him.*
>
> 1 Samuel 16: 14

> 2. *And the Philistines pursued Saul and his sons, and slew Jonathan and Abinadab and Malchi-shua, Saul's sons.*
> 6. *So Saul, his three sons, his armor bearer, and all his men died that day together.*
>
> 1 Samuel 31:2 &6

Outward Christianity portrays a life that has all the attractive appearances of success and also the outward picture of power but is lacking in real power and godly life on the inside.

An outward Christian has no life on the inside, no fire, no power. All he possesses is a casing of beauty. He looks spiritual and pious on the outside. He looks beautiful, shiny and all put together outside, but inside he is completely devoid of God's life. Inside him he breeds death, rottenness and the stench of death. All he has are outward effects.

Outward Christianity possesses all the shows and attributes of physical clout, physical power plus religious power, but is empty of Holy Ghost Power.

The passion for power is a legal human thing. Every human being craves power in one form or the other, at one level or the other. The desire for power in itself is not wrong. The question is: "What are the motives behind this desire? What kind of power do we want? Power over whom? Power over what? Power for what? Is the quest for power selfless or self-motivated?"

We need to be more concerned about what goes on in our inward or inner life, for that is our real life. Our emphasis should not be on the outer life or outward life.

The inner life speaks of the kind of relationship that exists between a person and God. Our inner life decides our standing with God, as opposed to our outer life that reflects our standing with the world and with people.

Our standing with God should be our priority and main concern. The state of our inner life should be more important to us than our outer life. Our inner life is where we are built so that we can lead meaningful and fulfilling lives on the outside. We are built from the inside on to the outside.

Our inner life is where God wants to possess and live in, so that He can reflect to the outer life. When our inner life is filled with God, our outer life will automatically display and reflect God.

Genuine power and prosperity come from God. As believers, our lives can only manifest God's genuine power and prosperity if we are truly cleansed from the inside and filled on the inside with God. When we focus on our outward lives and neglect our inward life, the bible calls us hypocrites.

13. *Woe to you, teachers of the law and Pharisees, you hypocrites! You shut the kingdom of heaven in men's faces. You yourselves do not enter, nor will you let those enter who are trying to.*

14. *Woe to you, teachers of the law and Pharisees, you hypocrites! You devour widows' houses and for a show make lengthy prayers. Therefore you will be punished more severely.*

15. *Woe to you, teachers of the law and Pharisees, you hypocrites! You travel over land and sea to win a single convert, and when he becomes one, you make him twice as much a son of hell as you are.*

16. *Woe to you, blind guides! You say, 'If anyone swears by the temple, it means nothing; but if anyone swears by the gold of the temple, he is bound by his oath.'*

17. *You blind fools! Which is greater: the gold, or the temple that makes the gold sacred?*

18. *You also say, 'If anyone swears by the altar, it means nothing; but if anyone swears by the gift on it, he is bound by his oath.'*

19. *You blind men! Which is greater: the gift, or the altar that makes the gift sacred?*

20. *Therefore, he who swears by the altar swears by it and by everything on it.*

21. *And he who swears by the temple swears by it and by the one who dwells in it.*

22. *And he who swears by heaven swears by God's throne and by the one who sits on it.*

23. *"Woe to you, teachers of the law and Pharisees, you hypocrites! You give a tenth of your spices - mint, dill and cummin. But you have neglected the more important matters of the law - justice, mercy and faithfulness. You should have practiced the latter, without neglecting the former.*

24. *You blind guides! You strain out a gnat but swallow a camel!*

25. *"Woe to you teachers of the law and Pharisees, you hypocrites! You clean the outside of the cup and dish, but inside they are full of greed and self-indulgence.*

Matthew 23:13-25

When we are clean from the inside, automatically our outward life will manifest this cleanliness. Inner cleansing is of the utmost importance in our walk with God.

> *Blind Pharisees! First clean the inside of the cup*
> *and dish, and then the outside also will be clean.*
>
> Matthew 23:26 NIV

When we desire to have a shiny, excellent life, then we should seek and strive to be cleansed inwardly. A clean inward life is a clean outward life. Inward cleansing comes about by taking in the Spirit of God and the Word of God into our spirits and living by the Spirit and the Word. The Word of God by the Spirit of God, active in the inward parts of a man, works cleansing.

> *How shall a young man cleanse his way? By*
> *taking heed and keeping watch [on himself]*
> *according to Your word [conforming his life to it].*
>
> Psalm 119:9

When the Holy Spirit is allowed to move on the Word of God in our heart, the cleansing is achieved in the inner self. When we have a deep relationship with God, we open our hearts to receive His word, because we sincerely desire to know Him. We read and study scriptures, we listen to the preached word, we read gospel materials. The Holy Spirit moves the Word of God in our inner self and cleanses us from all impurities, filth and inconsistencies.

> *You are cleansed and pruned already, because of*
> *the word which I have given you [the teachings I*
> *have discussed with you].*
>
> John 15:3

As we relate to God closely and intimately in His Word, the Word of God illuminates the darkness in our inner lives, and our inner lives are flooded with the light of God.

> *The entrance and unfolding of Your words give*
> *light.*
>
> Psalm 119:130a

The closer we get to God by abiding in His word constantly and consistently, the more we are changed by the Holy Spirit and we begin to look, talk and live like God.

> And all of us, as with unveiled face, [because
> we] continued to behold [in the Word of God]
> as in a mirror the glory of the Lord, are
> constantly being transfigured into His very
> own image in ever increasing splendor and
> from one degree of glory to another; [for this
> comes] from the Lord [Who is] the Spirit.
>
> 2 Corinthians 3:18

As people called by the name of God, we must not lose sight of the essence of the gospel. Why are we saved? - To be different, to make a difference, to reflect God to the world. We are saved to live by God's standard so that God can live His life in us; so that we can fellowship with God and bring others to Him. We need to keep in sight the fundamentals of Christianity. These fundamentals are taught at the level of our Christian foundation. We must never outgrow them or disregard their essence and value.

These fundamentals are the bedrock on which the whole of our Christian Spiritual life rests. They are essentials of salvation. We need to get back into them to see if we truly are still on the right track or we have derailed a little or completely.

No believer, no matter at what level of authority or position can live outside these fundamentals. They are the foundation of Christianity. Living outside them is not to live as a true believer in Christ Jesus.

Chapter Five

WHO IS SAVED?

Salvation in itself is from within. Salvation starts from deep within the soul and then radiates to the outside. It begins from the inside, the heart, and then reflects on the outside.

The Word of God says our soul (our inner being) had been defiled, corrupted and condemned before we became saved. We had darkened understanding and hard hearts (Ephesians 4:13). Our minds and consciences were defiled.

> *The Lord saw that the wickedness of man was great in the earth, and that every imagination and intention of all human thinking was only evil continually.*
>
> Genesis 6:5

> 16 *For God so greatly loved and dearly prized the world that He [even] gave up His only begotten (unique) Son, so that whoever*

believes in (trusts in, clings to, relies on)
Him shall not perish (come to destruction,
be lost) but have eternal (everlasting) life.

17 *For God did not send the Son into the world*
in order to judge (to reject, to condemn, to
pass sentence on) the world, but that the
world might find salvation and be made
safe and sound through Him.

John 3:16-17

Salvation is the saving grace of that soul (inner being) from darkness, defilement and condemnation. Salvation is an inner being action.

When we realize in ourselves that we need to turn from sin to God, we genuinely repent, that is, we have a change of attitude towards our wrong doings, towards sin, and then we turn to God; this is called REPENTANCE to life. We have made a CONSCIOUS effort on the inside of us to DEPART from sin and obtain CHRIST'S life within us. So, because we believe in our hearts in Christ's saving grace, we open our mouths to confess Jesus as our Lord and Saviour and we immediately receive Him into our HEARTS. - (Rom. 10:9 &10).

REGENERATION is a supernatural act of God. When we have confessed Jesus as our Lord and Saviour and we have invited Him into our hearts, a new work begins inside us. The Holy Spirit creates in and within us a new life. He gives us a

NEW NATURE. The old nature of sin, because it cannot be altered, is done away with. The old nature will not work in us a new work. A NEW NATURE is created inside us. This NEW NATURE is not the same as the old one. They are two distinctly different natures. The old nature goes out and the new nature comes in. The old is taken away completely and is now replaced by a new. The NEW NATURE is the nature of God Himself. This whole process is called regeneration. We have become new.

Now, there are three aspects of Salvation:
1. JUSTIFICATION
2. SANCTIFICATION
3. GLORIFICATION

1. JUSTIFICATION is God declaring righteous the believer. God uses His judicial action, to change the believer's standing. The believer's standing is completely changed from guilty and deserving of punishment to - not guilty, righteous and acceptable. Before now, because of our sins, we had been condemned and made unfit and unsuitable. But justification changes that condemnation to righteousness. Our status changes from condemned to justified. Grace finds us and declares us discharged, acquitted and accepted. Jesus imputes His own righteousness into us as a gift of grace. The believer is delivered from the position of sin.

2. SANCTIFICATION exhibits the fruits of a regenerated and justified life. Sanctification is what the Holy Spirit does inside us. Immediately we become born again, the Holy Spirit comes to live inside us. He then begins the work of separating us unto God to live a clean and holy life. Sanctification is separation. It is to be set apart by God for God. To be set apart from sin to a holy life. The Holy Spirit sets us apart for Himself so that we can live a clean life for Him.

> So whoever cleanses himself [from what is ignoble and unclean, who separates himself from contact with contaminating and corrupting influences] will [then himself] be a vessel set apart and useful for honorable and noble purposes, consecrated and profitable to the Master, fit and ready for any good work.
>
> 2 Timothy 2:21

We are separated from evil unto God. The moment we believe in Christ, we become sanctified. Sanctification is instantaneous at conversion and continues progressively through our Christian walk until complete; that is, until when we are made perfect in Christ Jesus.

We are converted to Christ; then as we read, believe, meditate and walk in the Word of God, our spots and blemishes (faults and mistakes) are revealed to us. We appropriate the blood of Jesus Christ to cleanse us from these blemishes (sin)

This means that as we see a spot (a fault, a sin), we do not hide it or ignore it. We want it removed, so we confess it and are cleansed immediately by the blood of Jesus Christ, and we are strengthened by the Holy Spirit not to go back to the fault/sin.

As we walk with God, He shows us our flaws and sometimes chastises and disciplines us for our own good. As we receive God's tutoring and discipline with the right heart attitude and as we strive to get better, we do begin to walk step by step and live day by day as God desires. We are progressively sanctified.

Sanctification is living a surrendered life. Every minute, every second we are walking in yielding to God. We are completely open before Him so that He can take away from us everything that will not please or honour Him, so that He can then use us for Himself.

> *I am speaking in familiar human terms because of your natural limitations. For as you yielded your bodily members [and faculties] as servants to impurity and ever increasing lawlessness, so now yield your bodily members [and faculties] once for all as servants to righteousness (right being and doing) [which leads] to sanctification.*
>
> Romans 6: 19

Sanctification comes by separating ourselves by the Power of the Holy Spirit from all that is unholy and unclean unto a Holy and clean God.

> *THEREFORE, SINCE these [great] promises are ours, beloved, let us cleanse ourselves from everything that contaminates and defiles body and spirit, and bring [our] consecration to completeness in the [reverential] fear of God.*
>
> 2 Corinthians 7:1

Sanctification involves making a deliberate, determined, individual effort to seek out sin in our lives and have it purged. We criticize ourselves closely and sincerely; we monitor ourselves by the mirror of the Word of God, thus, we are being delivered daily from the power of sin and we begin to look more like him every day.

We are always quick to cast away sin from our lives. We seek cleansing, and we diligently, earnestly pursue a path to progressive, daily (day-by-day, step-by-step) holy living.

We are sincere in this walk. As we abide in Him by obedience to the Word of God and continuous appropriation of the Saviour's life style, we enter into holy living by the power of the Holy Spirit.

3.   GLORIFICATION is the day when the standing of the believer and the present state of the believer become one. This

occurs at rapture or physical death – (departure from this world as a justified and sanctified believer). The believer finally keeps his date with the presence of God and God bestows perfected immortality on the believer. Sanctification is now perfected. Salvation is complete. The believer is completely delivered from the presence of sin.

So, regeneration changes our nature, then justification changes our standing and then sanctification PROGRESSIVELY changes our CHARACTER. In glorification we find perfection in Christ Jesus. Without regeneration there is no salvation. Without justification there is no salvation. So also without sanctification there is no salvation. With glorification, our salvation is perfected. Glorification changes us and makes us perfect the moment we enter into His presence.

When we become new creatures in Christ Jesus, we are made righteous before God and are transformed DAILY by the Holy Spirit and by the Word of God. We continue to grow holier by the day. Not by living by a set of dos and don'ts, but by walking with God in complete submission, transparency and in truth, minute-by-minute, day-by-day.

True salvation is portrayed in our CHARACTER. The things we do, think and say on A DAILY BASIS testify of our rebirth. By the things we think, say and do, we show we are who we claim to be.

No one born again can live a life full of sin. When we become born-again, we automatically have a new nature. This is the nature of the Holy God. This nature cannot practice sin.

A true believer cannot LIVE in unrighteousness, sexual immorality, wickedness, envy, murder, hatred, deceit, violence, pride, anger, malice, covetousness, greed, unforgiveness, lack of love, etc. A born again believer has a new heart, a new nature that cannot accommodate all these.

> *No one born (begotten) of God [deliberately, knowingly, and habitually] practices sin, for God's nature abides in him [His principle of life, the divine sperm, remains permanently within him]; and he cannot practice sinning because he is born (begotten) of God.*
>
> 1 John 3:9

He CANNOT practice sin, He CANNOT. Practice is repeated action or habitual performance. Any one action, activity, individual deed, exercise, operation, performance, and so on, done more than once, is a repeat, a practice.

When you PRACTICE sin of any kind: stealing, use of abusive language, slander, gossip, dirty talk, fornication, ill temper, selfishness, envy, trouble making, adultery, sexual immorality, you don't have a new nature. You are still operating the old nature. You are not regenerated. You are not saved. You are not born again.

True salvation must manifest in our behaviour. Our actions, thoughts and words must demonstrate our genuine repentance from sin and from the works of the flesh. When this is not so, we are not born again. We are not truly believers.

A saved life, a born-again believing Christian, is supposed to be a model. When you hear and see a believer, it should be that you hear and see God. A believer should be pure and undefiled in speech, in action and in appearance. Not yet perfect, but working and walking towards perfection.

Most believers are not any different from the world, in their utterances and behaviour. When provoked, they utter foul language, they curse, they slander. When up against the wall, their true un-regenerated nature manifests. There is no way a regenerated life will continue to speak profanities, utter filth or use coarse language.

8. *But now put away and rid yourselves [completely] of all these things; anger, rage, bad feeling towards others, curses and slander, and foulmouthed abuse and shameful utterances from your lips!*

9. *Do not lie to one another, for you have stripped off the old (unregenerate) self with its evil practices,*

10. *And have clothed yourselves with the new [spiritual self], which is [ever in the process of being] renewed and remolded into [fuller and more perfect knowledge upon]*

> *knowledge after the image (the likeness) of*
> *Him Who created it.*
>
> Colossians 3:8-10

A born again believer cannot live an insincere life. He is aware that he does not possess the power to live right, however God does, so he is transparent and communicative in his relationship with God. He recognizes and acknowledges the ugly manifestations of the flesh and he is quick to quell them by cooperating with the Holy Spirit. He will not excuse his faults. He moves earnestly to correct them. He acknowledges that he is imperfect and he is susceptible, but he seeks to work and walk with God to keep him out of trouble, so that he can progressively move into perfection.

Chapter Six

SLEEPING IN BONDAGE?

Aborn-again believer acknowledges his fleshly weaknesses (that is, the sins that easily beset him). He will not live by the dictates of his flesh, for he knows that by so doing he will become God's enemy.

> *For if you live according to [the dictates of] the flesh, you will surely die. But if through the power of the [Holy] Spirit you are [habitually] putting to death (making extinct, deadening) the [evil] deeds prompted by the body, you shall [really and genuinely] live forever.*
>
> Romans 8:13

He is zealous in his onslaught against these weaknesses. He puts these weaknesses before God and he desires to see them completely taken away.

Weaknesses are not to be idolized, nurtured or pampered. Weaknesses are not excuses for anyone to live a life of sin and carelessness.

We should not put our weaknesses on a pedestal and say, "Oh! You know, I am weak in this area; so you see I must be excused when I fall into sin," or "God Himself understands my weaknesses," or "You see, I cannot just help myself."

We should be violent against these weaknesses and seek to see them uprooted from our lives so we can manifest the nature of God that we have been given.

This new nature is a gift from God. To enjoy this gift, we must unwrap it, that is, open it up. This new nature cannot manifest unless we make a deliberate and conscious effort to open it up and use it. This is not our old nature, this is the nature of God.

For example, a new pair of high heeled shoes for someone who has never worn heels before would be quite a struggle initially. It would take some getting used to. The person would most likely stumble a little, falter a bit, wobble, trip up and might even fall flat, but soon enough, with regular, constant, consistent walking in the high heels, it would soon become second nature.

The nature we have been given must be allowed to manifest. We must not allow weaknesses, laziness, the attractions of the world, to stifle out or strangulate the nature of God in us. It is our choice. The nature is a new one that we are not used to, but we can allow the Holy Spirit by the word of God, to help us live God's nature out one day at a time until we get used to living that way. If we go back to what we are used to, we will gradually push aside and eventually push out this

39

gift we were given at new birth. Perfection is given to us at new birth in Christ; we grow into it as we walk with Him a step at a time, a day at a time until we are made perfect at the end.

We should violently attack fleshly manifestations to see them completely obliterated. If we do not wage war against them to destroy them, they will ultimately destroy us.

Fleshly weaknesses that are not dealt with at the right time will wait patiently like a cancer for a time in future to rear their ugly heads and strike to bring public shame and humiliation and destruction.

Weaknesses are no reasons for sin and immorality. Weaknesses are not supposed to be indulged or nursed. They are not supposed to be swept under the carpet and kept away from sight. Some day they will struggle free from concealment at the least expected time to cause unimaginable embarrassment and reproach. Weaknesses should be vehemently opposed and seriously dealt with. Everyone is faced with one fleshly weakness or the other. But notwithstanding, weaknesses must not be given room to manifest over and over again.

If we truly possess a NEW NATURE (the nature of God), then we will live the sanctified life. This is a life that yields to God and is led by the Spirit of God. A life that sees sin, confesses it immediately and seeks cleansing from it. A life that is willing to part from sin and from every form of filth and uncleanliness.

This daily Christian walk with God is a CONSCIOUS effort to stay away from everything called sin. Our lives must be DISCIPLINED and completely ruled by God's Word and God's Spirit.

We must live a life of daily consecration, then we are more sanctified as each day goes by. We move from one level of glory to the other in our inner lives by the Holy Spirit.

> *And all of us, as with unveiled face, [because we] continued to behold [in the word of God] as in a mirror the glory of the Lord, are constantly being transfigured into His very own image in ever increasing splendor and from one degree of glory to another; [for this comes] from the Lord [Who is] the Spirit.*
>
> 2 Corinthians 3:18

> *But the path of the [uncompromisingly] just and righteous is like the light of dawn, that shines more and more (brighter and clearer) until [it reaches its full strength and glory in] the perfect day [to be prepared].*
>
> Proverbs 4:18

No man can by his own power make himself clean. Our righteousness is not by our works.

But people are counted righteous, not because of their work, but because of their faith in God who forgives sinners.

Romans 4:5 (NLT)

We still live in the flesh so we are still susceptible to errors, faults, and failings. We sometimes fall, but we are not to stay down.

If we truly desire change, if we truly desire to live a sanctified life, when we discover and detect these fleshly manifestations, we must lean completely on the power of the Holy Spirit. If we are sincerely willing, He will help us deal with them and transform us. When we give these weaknesses to God, He will immediately start a work of forgiveness and cleansing in us.

When, most importantly, we stay away from those things that cause us to fall, then we can move forward steadily in righteousness in God.

We must also be careful that we make no provisions for the flesh.

We repent genuinely from our sins, we desire to and work at staying away from these sins. We do not remain in our sins, nor do we move backward into decadence.

We should not sit and continue to live in weakness, but we get up and appropriate God's strength and we live in this strength step-by-step and day-by-day.

We are supposed to live a life free from the chains of sin and darkness. Sin is bondage, sin chains, sin traps. We, by Jesus Christ, have been set free, so we should live a life that portrays and reflects this freedom. We are set free to STAND straight and tall in liberty. We should stop sitting and sleeping in bondage.

> *Stand fast therefore in the liberty by which Christ has made us free, and do not be entangled again with a yoke of bondage.*
>
> Galatians 5:1 NKJV

When fleshly weaknesses rear their ugly heads in our lives to lead us to temptation, we should quell them by standing firm in the strength of God by His word and His Spirit. We should stand and not bend or fall. God is more than able and also willing to help us stand if only we are willing to stand.

Temptation is not sin. It is the way we respond/react to temptations that leads either to sin or not. Everyone desiring holiness will definitely face and experience temptations. Temptation to display anger, to engage in sexual immorality, to lie, to steal, to gossip, to use foul language, and so on.

Temptation is fashioned to lead us away from God's designed plan and purpose for our lives. God's plans for us are plans of blessings and goodness.

For I know the plans I have for you," declares the LORD, "plans to prosper you and not to harm you, plans to give you hope and a future.

Jeremiah 29:11 NIV

The devil, just like he did to Adam and Eve in the garden is still doing to man on a daily basis. He wants us to fall short of God's best for us. He is still using his wiles to use man's weaknesses against man.

Temptations are supposed to be ladders to our lifting. Temptations should make us stronger not weaker. Temptations should strengthen our walk with God.

We always have a choice when we are tempted. We either fall into temptation or run from it. If our destiny is more important to us than the brief pleasures of satisfying our flesh, we will resist temptations. If our destiny means little or nothing to us, we will close our eyes to the consequences and yield to temptation.

One man esteemed his destiny above momentary pleasure. He valued his destiny above brief satisfaction of physical cravings and physical desires. He fled from temptation and for this reason he rose to be the most powerful man of his time.

When you flee from temptation, you rise to promotion and prominence and to destiny fulfillment.

Joseph did not succumb to Mrs. Potiphar's lustful advances. As a full-grown man, he must have felt some stirrings when she tried to entice him. For, she caught him by his garment, which suggests that she had him close enough to touch. But Joseph was locked in his desire to live a sanctified life. His future was more important to Him. He would not sin against his God. He was tempted but he did not yield, he did not fall, he did not sin.

7. *Then after a time his master's wife cast her eyes upon Joseph, and she said, Lie with me.*

8. *But he refused and said to his master's wife, See here, with me in the house my master has concern about nothing; he has put all that he has in my care.*

9. *He is not greater in this house than I am; nor has he kept anything from me except you, for you are his wife. How the can I do this great evil and sin against God?*

10. *She spoke to Joseph day after day, but he did not listen to her, to lie with her or to be with her.*

11. *Then it happened about this time that Joseph went into the house to attend to his duties, and none of the men of the house were indoors.*

12. *And she caught him by his garment, saying, Lie with me! But he left his garment in her*

hand and fled and got out [of the house].
Genesis 39:7-12

We have the choice and also the ability to refuse temptations if and when they come.

No temptation has seized you except what is common to man. And God is faithful; he will not let you be tempted beyond what you can bear. But when you are tempted, he will also provide a way out so that you can stand up under it.
1 Corinthians 10:13 NIV

When we fall into temptation, it is not because there is no way of escape or because the temptation is too strong. We fall because WE CHOOSE to follow our flesh. This is a deliberate purposeful choice; it is not an accident or a mistake. It is a willful choice that we make.

There is always an escape route for us when we are tempted. When we refuse temptation, we are strengthened in our walk with God. God in turn rewards us in due season. When we choose not to refuse temptation and we succumb to it, it is then that we sin and receive due recompense.

12. Blessed is the man who perseveres under trial, because when he has stood the test, he will receive the crown of life that God has promised to those who love him.

13. When tempted, no one should say, "God is tempting me." For God cannot be tempted by evil, nor does he tempt anyone;

14. But each one is tempted when, by his own evil desire, he is dragged away and enticed.

15. Then, after desire has conceived, it gives birth to sin; and sin, when it is full-grown, gives birth to death.

16. Don't be deceived, my dear brothers.

James 1:12-16 NIV

7. Do not be deceived and deluded and misled; God will not allow Himself to be sneered at (scorned, disdained or mocked by mere pretensions or professions, or by His percepts being set aside). [He inevitably deludes himself who attempts to delude God.] For whatever a man sows, that and that only is what he will reap.

8a. For he who sows to his own flesh (lower nature, sensuality) will from the flesh reap decay and ruin and destruction, but he who sows in the Spirit will from the Spirit reap eternal life.

Galatians 6:7-8a

Short-sightedness is what makes us fall into sin when we are tempted. We focus only on the here and now. We need to begin to look beyond the momentary pleasure, satisfaction or gratification of our flesh and our emotions. We need to project farther than the present circumstances and present needs. We must always think beyond the now. We must always consider the future.

Chapter Seven

WALTER MAKOVA

Walter Makova's colleagues had all gone out to lunch. He was not hungry.

Besides, he could barely afford to eat today. He had had lunch two afternoons already this week and that was all his pay packet could accommodate - lunch two afternoons a week.

It was just six days into the new month and he was already anticipating eagerly his next pay cheque. He had outstanding bills to clear. He had unpaid pledges in church; he had not completed payment on his monthly house rent; his mother had not received her weekly allowance from him in six weeks now.

"Hey! What are you doing here all by yourself boy? Planning on how to rob the bank?" Walter had not heard Nicholas, the office accountant, come up behind him.

"Rob the bank?" Walter exclaimed, "My goodness! Not in a million years; my God is no thief, therefore I cannot steal."

"Aw! Common!" Nicholas continued, "That was just a joke! Anyway, come on, let's go for lunch; my treat!"

All of a sudden Walter's stomach growled. Funny! So he was hungry after all.

"Thanks pal!" He said, as he got up and hurriedly tidied up his desk to follow after his friend.

* * *

Traffic was so bad tonight. They had been stuck out here for an hour and a half. Walter knew he still had at least another one hour to get home. The bus was hot and stuffy, people were exhausted and tempers were at an all-time high.

Amidst the hue and cry, he sat quietly in his corner by the window and prayed silently. "Oh God, please help me and reward my faithfulness. Give me a car of my own, change my accommodation, give me a new life, I need a change."

When they had gotten off work today, almost all of Walter's colleagues got into their own cars and headed towards the 'traffic free zone' on the Island. He had hopped on a bus going into heavy traffic in the opposite direction.

"When will my change come?" Walter muttered softly to himself. "God's word says "now!" is the time. My change must come now!" He could not continue to be a failure. He would not continue to be less than his peers. He had to become somebody. He had to move up in life.

When he had first landed this bank job, people had applauded him, congratulated him and rejoiced with him. He had enjoyed the admiration and respect of his church and neighbourhood. But now, after two years at the bank, he still had no car, no new apartment of his own. His material and financial status were nothing to celebrate. He had soon discovered that people were not as warm towards him as they used to be. His pastor had advised him to go on a thirty-day fast, which he had done with his whole heart and might. Yet nothing had changed. He was now so frustrated and so unhappy.

Walter shifted his eyes to the man sitting beside him, obviously a man who works with his hands. His hands were calloused and rough. He clothes were worn, and filthy. His arms were thick and looked as if they could do physical damage. He thought about his friends now, probably relaxing at home with a glass of cold juice in their air-conditioned and cool apartments. But here he was, forced to mingle with people like this.

Walter's eyes returned from their trip to the rough-looking thug. "Now is the time! My change must come now!" Tomorrow he would apply for an international travelling passport.

* * *

"Walter! The Queen's boy! So when are you leaving us?" asked Nicholas.

"Why do you talk like I am never coming back? I am only going on a two-week vacation you know," retorted Walter.

"You could have fooled me there for a second," sniggered Nicholas; "we all know when you leave these shores; if you ever come back it would be a miracle."

"Well then get ready, for that's one miracle you are sure to see," Walter responded.

All plans were concluded for Walter's trip. Working in the bank had at least secured for him a three-month visiting visa to the United Kingdom. His pastor had been ecstatic when he shared his travelling plans and a three-day fast and fervent prayer session had been quickly organized to facilitate his visa approval. One thing Walter could not get over though was Pastor Haname - the assistant pastor's lack of enthusiasm at his plans. Haname insisted that he was sure God wanted Walter to stay on at the Bank.

"Stay on at the bank!" That was incredulous. What on earth for? God would never want him to wallow in poverty while all his friends and colleagues were moving ahead and making it in life. God had no such backward, relegating plans for him, he was sure. Haname was just being over-spiritual as usual. That was exactly what he had done when Charles Elukan told the church that he had received God's call on his life to start a church on the highbrow Peninsula on the Island. Pastor Haname had asked Charles to go and spend more time seeking the face of God before stepping out. The boy had foolishly consented and the result was that now Charles was in his father's village, doing missionary work. Ah! When he could have been counting his millions as a big pastor on the

Peninsula. Worse still, the poor deluded boy keeps telling people in that poverty-ridden state of his that he is fulfilled. Indeed!

Walter knew that as for him, this was his own time to move on and make it big. God does not back losers. God had proven to him that his time is 'NOW'! Nicholas had been too willing to help substitute Walters name for a wealthy bank customer's, on the customer's bank statement. This, Walter had produced at the visa office for his visa application. "God is a good God." Nicholas had helped Walter again by "loaning" him half a million from an unsuspecting customer's account. This was surely divine favour. Walter certainly believed that the cloak that had been covering his destiny and keeping it from manifesting greatness had just been lifted. His pastor testified to this.

Walter would stay on and work in the United Kingdom for about three years, but first, he must immediately seek to get married to a Briton (an elderly and rich one preferably). By the time he finally returns to Nigeria, he knows the glory of God would be all over him. He would be able to afford all his heart desires and live the life befitting a child of God. "God is indeed a good God."

Chapter Eight

Satisfying The Hunger Deep Within

As Christians, our fervent quest for fame, power, authority, and riches is what makes us outward Christians. This desire in itself speaks of something.

As created beings, we possess a legal hunger and thirst. We are innately hungry and thirsty beings. We have a natural craving inside us itching for satisfaction. As human beings we long for fulfillment.

We want to be successful in life. No one wants to be a failure. Everyone wants to feel and have a sense of achievement. This in itself is not wrong at all. There is a God given hunger for excellence in every living man. The error is in when we believe success is measured by physical accomplishments.

When we seek to fulfill ourselves without waiting on God to lead and guide us into what He wants for us, we are chasing after lustful desires.

We look to physical things to give us the contentment and satisfaction that we so greatly need. We think we can find happiness and fulfillment in people or in things. We think we can find fulfillment in marriage or in child bearing.

We think we can derive joy from a bigger, better, house or car. We look and seek for more fantastic jobs with huge paychecks. We even think close companionship or understanding friendship with others, will do it for us.

People and things will fail us. For all these can never truly satisfy and fulfill the deep cravings and longings of our souls.

Sometimes our desires even seem noble and virtuous. We want to work for God. We want to do ministry. We fast, we pray, we go through all the motions. We work hard. We build. We travel far and wide for crusades and revivals; but in all this that we do, we are fired up by the desire to be successful, rich and glamorous.

We strive to have ministry branches in every town, in every city. We conduct deliverance services, healing and miracle meetings. We study scriptures, we teach mysteries, and we hunger and search for new insights; but still our focus is on self actualization. We want acclaim, we want fame. We do not possess the life of God on the inside of us.

37. And the Father who sent me has himself testified concerning me. You have never heard his voice nor seen his form,

38. Nor does his word dwell in you, for you do not believe the one he sent.

> 39. *You diligently study the Scriptures because you think that by them you possess eternal life. These are the Scriptures that testify about me.*
>
> 40. *Yet you refuse to come to me to have life.*
>
> John 5:37-40 NIV

We do not have the life of God inside of us. We do all that we do to gratify ourselves. It is all in our quest for fame, power, and wealth that we seek all we seek in ministry. We use the work of the ministry to bring ourselves into fame, wealth and power. Our concentration is on who and what we want to be. We use the gospel of Jesus Christ for our own self-actualization. We are motivated in ministry because of our own self-centered desires and goals, not because of selfless service to God and His people.

We expend all our energies in planning and praying to God for the things "we need". We search the scriptures for "keys to MY success and prosperity," "20 ways to MY abundance," "3 ways to MY millions."

We have the scriptures to quote and mediate upon for favour, for blessings, and for breakthrough; all for self-prominence and self-gratification. We seek all we seek in God for self and self. We search for power; power to do miracles, power to heal, power to acquire, power to manipulate men. We spend much time in prayers, we 'diligently' study scriptures, we read, we listen; all for SELF.

We study successful life styles. We go to meetings to observe the Set Man's style, his method and his formula. We use these men as points of contact. We struggle to be like them.

In all this, all that we desire is the physical outward gains of power, wealth, and fame. All that we aim for and strive for is to please ourselves. All we desire is to be translated into material wealth, material gains and comforts, so that we can consume it all on ourselves and so that we can be applauded and celebrated by men. This shows we are nothing but outward Christians.

True power springs forth from inner cleanliness. Inner cleanliness is what fills a man's life with the power of God Most High. Inner cleansing is the work of the Holy Spirit. No man can cleanse himself. The Holy Spirit cleanses us if and when we allow Him to.

When the Holy Spirit is in-dwelling and He is in full control of our inner lives, He will give us the power to live a prosperous and blessed life.

God created us for His fellowship. We can only be content and satisfy the longings of our soul when we are in intimate fellowship with Him. Our desires should be solely purely for God and for more of Him.

It is all right to want things. There is absolutely nothing wrong in wanting a better life, a more comfortable and peaceful existence. It is when we want things outside God that it becomes destructive to us.

All the things we want must be channeled through God. That is, we want God first, then we want all the things He wants for us. We do not want less than God wants for us, nor do we want more than He wants for us. We must not have a desire that is above Him, stronger than Him or outside of Him.

When we live in God's presence, we will find out that our deepest longings are fully satisfied in Him. When we are concerned about nothing else but a deep one on one, transparent communion with God; when all we seek is true, intimate, habitual fellowship with Him, we will find everything we need for physical living being given to us without our having to labour, sweat or struggle to get them. He will satisfy all our needs and we will not have wants outside Him.

The hunger deep in our souls can only be truly satisfied by God. The vacuum we are seeking to fill with material things can only be properly filled by the presence of God Himself.

We are created to need God. We are created to pant for God. There is a deep hunger and a deep thirst on the inside of each one of us. This deep longing can only be filled and satiated by God.

And my God will liberally supply (fill to the full) your every need according to His riches in glory in Christ Jesus.

Philippians 4:19

Chapter Nine

THESPIS AND RHOAHAMAH ABRAHAM

It was a cool, clear and beautiful morning, the hand woven Bulgarian cotton curtains of the family lounge billowed ever so softly in the gentle fragrant breeze that wafted in from the garden. Rhoahamah Naomi Abraham was seated in her favourite leather backed, ornately carved, high royal chair, delicately sipping an exotic blend of Brazilian and Turkish coffee and staring at the front pages of the day's newspapers that lay beside her coffee service. Seated across the coffee table was Jonah Birding, senior special personal assistant and major domo to the Bishop Mrs.

Rhoahamah looked up at Jonah and said, "Sometimes life throws you giant bricks... some you dodge, but some just don't miss... and if you're like me, you pick them up, you get cracking and build palatial mansions with them. This latest scandal is news today, but by tomorrow morning those blood thirsty news-hounds must have found another juicy bit of flesh to sink their poisonous fangs into and devour for all I care, do I make myself clear?!".

"Yes, yes your eminence", Jonah answered, stuttering.

Rhoahamah sighed... "I know being the matriarch of a dynasty this prominent and this successful is not a walk in the park, but that does not mean that I will let this brouhaha get under my skin and smudge my mascara. If Thespis insists on being a total dolt, I really cannot be bothered, but I will not allow him to drag me or the children into his murky waters, neither will I let him defile all we have laboured for these many years."

Jonah made a little movement in his seat and started to study his finger nails with deep interest.

Rhoahamah undaunted, determined to spill her guts, continued in her cold and haughty voice; "If I could manage to keep the press and the world away for these past 16yrs from those two money sucking bugs he calls baby mamas and from all his other despicabilities, then I can do this also. How could he be so blind again? Did he not know that you do not dine with such off-springs of donkeys, if you do not have a protracted fork? He should have known they would have the whole meeting video tapped... Why must I keep doing his dry cleaning for him? Thousands of dollars again to quench his bushfire! This man is indeed an exasperating husband to me. Humph!"

Rhoahamah gracefully lifted the '1759 Wedgewood' coffee cup to her lips and sipped her rich dark brew as the day's 'sizzling hot' news cooled rapidly on her coffee table.

* * *

Walking out from the Red room where the gentle but strong humming voices of the intercessors filtered out, Adam Thespis Abraham with his head bowed and his temple furrowed walked across the hall towards his office. The plush and opulent carpet muffled the sounds of his footsteps... and that was how (before he turned the corner to his office), he overheard the female Deacon in charge of welfare talking to his trusted secretary of 8 years.

"Did the Archbishop really kneel before President Pracloco?", Deacon Marshall asked, ...

"Oh yes, he definitely did," replied Breena excitedly. She lowered her tone conspiratorially and continued, "I even heard that by the time the second duffel bag of American dollars was handed to him, he went flat on his face in appreciation and in awe, although he later claimed that it was in worship of God and not in any form of genuflection to a man."

Archbishop Thespis Abraham squared his shoulders and then calmly walked out from the hall corner and past the gossiping females as they gasped and slinked away hurriedly.

"What exactly did they expect of him? They have little or no understanding of kingdom dynamics. God had in His infinite mercy made him a minister to the rich and mighty, especially to the leading political power of the day. That was not a feat he achieved by himself. He had always known he was a prophet to the nations. And what better nation than his own. This was the Lord's doing and it is indeed marvellous. If Elisha had lived in these present times, he would not expect the kings to come and see him in his house, is it not written, "Since the days of John the Baptist, the kingdom of God suffereth violence and only the violent take it by force"? If one did not take by force, how else would the riches of the gentiles come into the hands of the saints? If the saints are not proactive they would die in poverty and in obscurity. We need to get up and go get it. We need to be wise like serpents. Mammon is a tool in the hands of believers. We will use it to lift the name of God. This wealth should be in the hands of God's children, its our right! God had been faithful, He had used this same riches of the gentiles to build for him a 150,000 seater, glass and marble cathedral as the church head quarters.

They had expanded to various cities of the major countries of the world. They had a cruiser liner, two (2) Leah jets, innumerable befitting state of the art vehicles and now they were ready to complete their very own Zion City on the beautiful Island of Tashishiva. The church is marching on and the gates of hell cannot prevail. This latest scandal is clearly the ugliness of the enemy rearing its head, he refuses to be bothered by it, it will not last forever, for the saints will crush the head of the enemy and victory will ultimately belong to the people of God. Away with their ignorance, they knoweth nothing!"

Chapter Ten

A FORM OF GODLINESS

When we are fully submitted to God in our inner lives we will receive empowerment for abundance in every area of our lives. When we are fully surrendered to Him to conform to His desires, He will manifest His power through our lives.

It is what we have on our insides that will reflect to the outside. The life we live inside will determine the life we will live on the outside.

When our inner life is full of God, then God's power will fill our inner life and will manifest in our outer life. When we open ourselves on the inside for God to have deep fellowship with us, He will manifest in our physical and outer lives also.

The devil will always have an advantage over us, if all we have on our minds is how to live in wealth, power, and abundance and in physical fulfillment. Our most important desire must be to fellowship intimately with God, no matter what.

Our hearts must be set on God, not on earthly pleasures. When we have a deep intimate relationship with God, He will take care of all our earthly concerns.

Anybody can be wealthy; hardworking bank executives, business executives, shipping magnates, hired guns, politicians, oil magnates, armed robbers, fraudsters, drug barons, teachers, and market traders, motor spare part dealers, anybody.

Anybody can acquire wealth. People acquire wealth by different means and different methods - connections, fraud, hard work, and inheritance and so on.

Anybody can be in a position of authority and power. Power, wealth, position, fame can come to anybody. The fact that you have riches and affluence does not make you a righteous person, it does not mean you are pleasing God.

The fact that a person who claims to be a preacher of the gospel acquires fame and wealth does not automatically mean that he is pleasing God or doing the will of God. It is not everything that looks good that is God. Even Satan is able to transform into an angel of light.

12. *But what I do, I will continue to do, [for I am determined to maintain this independence] in order to cut off the claim of those who would like [to find an occasion and incentive] to claim that in their boasted [mission] they work on the same terms that we do.*

13. *For such men are false apostles [spurious, counterfeits], deceitful workmen,*

> *masquerading as apostles (special*
> *messengers) of Christ (the Messiah).*
>
> 14. *And it is no wonder, for Satan himself*
>   *masquerades as an angel of light.*
> 15. *So it is not surprising if his servants also*
>   *masquerade as ministers of righteousness.*
>   *[But] their end will correspond with their*
>   *deeds.*
>
> 2 Corinthians 11:12-15

The fact that a ministry is booming with wealth and outward presentations of affluence is not a clear-cut signal that God approves of the minister in charge or of the ministry. The results he is getting are not infallible proofs of God's presence in that work. Anybody can acquire power, fame and wealth.

Miracles, 'signs and wonders,' DO NOT also always mean that God is in the house. After Samson was back-slidden and he had broken his consecration as a Nazarite, he still had several manifestations of the anointing of God upon him (Judges 14).

A particular time, he even rose from the bed of a harlot and still went on to manifest his awesome gift of strength, even though the presence of God had departed from his life a long time ago. The fire of God within him had died way back.

It was only a matter of time before the emptiness in Samson's inner life manifested on the outside. But before the "lack of the life of God" that was really on the inside of

Samson manifested on the outside he still had a show of might in his outward life.

Manifestations of the gift of God, material wealth, affluence, etc., do not always connote or constitute the power of the living God. When God gives you His gifts, He does not take them back.

> *For the gifts and calling of God are without repentance.*
>
> Romans 11:29 KJV

The gifts might become devoid of His presence when we walk out of fellowship with Him, but He does not take back the gifts. Again, it is not all miracles, signs and wonders that are from God.

9. *But there was a man named Simon, who had formerly practiced magic arts in the city to the utter amazement of the Samaritan nation, claiming that he himself was an extraordinary and distinguished person.*

10. *They all paid earnest attention to him, from the least to the greatest, saying, This man is that exhibition of the power of God which is called great (intense).*

11. *And they were attentive and made much of him, because for a long time he had amazed*

and bewildered and dazzled them with his skill in magic arts.

16. *However, when Simon saw that the [Holy] Spirit was imparted through the laying on of the apostles' hands, he brought money and offered it to them,*

17. *Saying, Grant me also this power and authority, in order that anyone on whom I place my hands may receive the Holy Spirit.*

18. *But Peter said to him, Destruction overtake your money and you, because you imagined you could obtain the [free] gift of God with money.*

19. *You have neither part nor lot in this matter, for your heart is all wrong in God's sight [it is not straightforward or right or true before God].*

20. *So repent of this depravity and wickedness of yours and pray to the Lord that, if possible, this contriving thought and purpose of your heart may be removed and disregarded and forgiven you.*

21. *For I see that you are in the gall of bitterness and in a bond forged by iniquity [to fetter souls].*

Acts 8:9-11, 18-23 (Emphasis added)

We must not confuse magic arts, occultism and spiritism with the power of God. These are rife now in our religious circles. Many of our celebrated religious leaders have veered into occultism and spiritism in a bid to "get results" to excite and entice the people. They have gone after "spiritual powers" that are not found in righteousness, all in a bid to acquire fame, power, wealth, etc.

Engaging the spirit world outside of the Holy Spirit and outside of the will of God is evil. Using spiritism to get results that will satisfy the cravings and the desires of the world's standard is demonology. Unrighteousness cannot work the will of God.

Where sin is PRACTICED at any level, no matter how seemingly minute - God is not a part of it.

Where lies, gossip, malice, any form of sexual immorality [(pornography - soft or hard), fondling of the opposite sex outside marriage], hypocrisy, and envy is PRACTICED, God's power cannot manifest there. God is Holy and His eyes cannot behold sin neither can He abide with ungodliness of any kind.

You are of purer eyes than to behold evil and cannot look [inactively] upon injustice.
                                        Habakkuk 1:13a

Most times, before we become outward Christians, we would have started our Christian walk well. In the beginning we were dedicated and our Christian walk was governed by the fundamentals of salvation.

But then as time goes on, our focus starts to shift. Sometimes this happens due to our exposure to erroneous teachings. For example, "we are saved to acquire riches and if we are not rich, then we must be doing something wrong."

The shift in focus could also be because we begin to look on the distractions of life. Like in the parable of the sower, "the worries of this life, the lure of wealth, and the desire for other things" (Mark 4: 19NLT) crowds out of us the solid teachings we had received. We look on the "boisterous winds" and our hearts begin to falter. We allow the storms of life to dictate to us how to live. Our hearts and minds are touched by trials and tribulations, and we are turned out of the way. We allow situations and circumstances to affect us negatively and we give in to wrong living.

We see people all around us living in affluence and plenty. We begin to compare ourselves and our lives with others and we see our "limitations" and "inadequacies." We do not want "life to pass us by." An intense desire for material comfort and improved circumstances wells up in us. Our EYES OPEN to all the things we do not have but which we want.

Then the eye of them both were opened, and they knew that they were naked; and they sewed fig leaves together and made themselves apronlike girdles

Genesis 3:7

Self-gratification or self-indulgence is a great destroyer of man's destiny. When we lose our focus on God and we concentrate on 'self' and its needs, then we are drawn away from God's plan and purpose for us, and invariably from His best for us. As a result of the fact that nations and communities are speaking of economic instability and recession, when we allow our needs and the desire for improved living conditions to get us carried away, we will fall below God's expectation for our lives and then we will begin to live a decadent life.

It is not wrong or sinful in itself to want improved circumstances. It is not sinful at all to desire a good life, but the main focus and goal in life must not be acquisition of material and financial comfort. Acquisition of material and financial resources is not the goal of our existence.

When we are under the influence of a passion for a better standard of life, we begin to equate success in life and ministry to fame, riches, power, affluence and the likes. We say we know God wants us to prosper, so we badger and harass Him with endless pleas and requests for prosperity, blessings and abundance. We seek earthly riches and treasures with our whole hearts and minds. We are tenacious and aggressive in our pursuit of material and physical blessings.

1. *If then you have been raised with Christ [to a new life, thus sharing His resurrection from the dead], aim at and seek the [rich, eternal treasures] that are above where Christ is, seated at the right hand of God.*
2. *And set your minds and keep them set on what is above (the higher things), not on the things that are on the earth.*
3. *For [as far as this world is concerned] you have died, and your [new, real] life is hidden with Christ in God.*

Colossians 3:1-3

When we are eaten up with the desires of self, the life of God is gradually choked out from our insides (Mark 4:19). Once this begins to happen, we begin to die on the inside. Unfortunately, most times when this dying process is going on we are not aware of the tragedy, this gradual loss of life. We carry on like we are still on course. We believe we are still in the will of God.

But now we are backslidden. We have become greedy and self-indulgent.

Our hearts, our inner lives, no longer beat and pant for intimate fellowship with God. We are now CONSUMED with the desire to be rich, the desire to prosper, and the desire to be "somebody."

Intimacy with the Holy Spirit is replaced with a strong will and determination to be a 'success.' Yes! We pray, sometimes even harder than before. The whole essence of Christianity now becomes, 'the man who gets the bigger and better results in riches, power and fame is the man who is the better believer.'

We use spiritual gifts to attract acclaim, riches and power. We advertise "signs, wonders and miracles". We study scriptures diligently to discover 'revelations' that will impress and dazzle the people. We clamour for applause and ovation. We strive to increase in knowledge so we can receive approval of men. We are no longer hungry for God's approval.

> *Do your best to present yourself to God as one approved, a workman who does not need to be ashamed and who correctly handles the word of truth.*
>
> 2 Timothy 2:15 NIV

The fire of God on the inside has been doused and replaced by the fire of the cravings of the flesh, the physical gratification of the better life. The main focus and joy of our life now is wealth and power. Paul had this to say concerning such.

> *17. Brethren, together follow my example and observe those who live after the pattern we have set for you.*

18. *For there are many, of whom I have often told you and now tell you even with tears, who walk (live) as enemies of the cross of Christ (the Anointed One).*

19. *They are doomed and their fate is eternal mystery (perdition); their god is their stomach (their appetites, their sensuality) and they glory in their shame, siding with earthly things and being of their party.*

Philippians 3:17-19

The lustful desires of the heart for physical wealth have broken down the defenses of the spirit. It is now easy to excuse "little sins." These slip-ups here and there come with the physical gratification territory.

9. *But those who crave to be rich fall into temptation and a snare and into many foolish (useless, godless) and hurtful desires that plunge men into ruin and destruction and miserable perishing.*

10. *For the Love of money is a root of all evils; it is through this carving that some have been led astray and have wandered from the faith and pierced themselves through with many acute [mental] pangs.*

1 Timothy 6:9-10

There is no longer the fear of God. We believe it is okay to sin in secret as long as no one can see. "It is only God who sees in secret; men do not." It is okay to fall into these secret sins so long as no one is caught. "After all, no man is entirely without sin." We label those who pant after God and are reluctant to fall into these fleshly traps as "over righteous" believers.

We compose special prayers and master the scriptures that guarantee us forgiveness and cleansing until our next indiscretion. We operate under 'a special grace.' "After all," we say, "at this level of ministry there is a peculiar grace that excuses certain sins." 'Grace' covers them.

This 'grace' is a foreign one; it is the false 'grace' which Jude warned about in (Jude 3-4).

3. *Dear friends, although I was very eager to write to you about the salvation we share, I felt I had to write and urge you to contend for the faith that was once for all entrusted to the saints.*

4. *For certain men whose condemnation was written about long ago have secretly slipped in among you. They are godless men, who change the grace of our God into a license for immorality and deny Jesus Christ our only Sovereign and Lord.*

Jude 3-4 NIV (Emphasis added)

Under such lives, such ministries, such titles, such big structures and big crusades, there is every manner of rottenness, stench and filth known to man. We walk and prance around in majestic garbs of charismatic arrogance and ministerial opulence but we are actually stinking dead bodies. Every form of immorality, filth and uncleanness exists under our sparkling robes. Every form of manipulation, depravity, deception is stored in our minds. There is double-dealing, backstabbing, greed and self-indulgence of every kind under our sparkling cloaks of brilliant colours. WHITEWASHED TOMBS FILLED WITH DEAD MEN'S BONES.

> 25. *Woe to you, scribes and Pharisees, pretenders (hypocrites)! For you clean the outside of the cup and of the plate, but within they are full of extortion (prey, spoil, plunder) and grasping self-indulgence.*
> 26. *You blind Pharisee! First clean the inside of the cup and of the plate, so that the outside may be clean also.*
> 27. *Woe to you, scribes and Pharisees, pretenders (hypocrites)! For you are like tombs that have been whitewashed, which look beautiful on the outside but inside are full of dead men's bones and everything impure.*

> 28. *Just so, you also outwardly seem to people to be just and upright but inside you are full of pretense and lawlessness and iniquity.*
>
> 33. *You serpents! You spawn of vipers! How can you escape the penalty to be suffered in hell (Gehenna)?*
>
> Matthew 23: 25-28, 33

We do not know that the fact that God is using a person mightily is not a clear cut sign that God approves of and (or) supports that person's lifestyle.

A styrofoam cup (disposable cup) is very useful. It can be used to hold any kind of beverage, from water, to tea, coffee, cocoa, juice, carbonated drinks, wine, spirits, and every kind of drink at whatever temperature.

Though it is a very useful vessel, it is not a vessel of honour. After use it is only fit for the garbage can. After use, it is disposed of.

> 22. *Many will say to me on that day, Lord, Lord, have we not prophesied in your name and driven out demons in Your name and done mighty works in Your name?*
>
> 23. *And then I will say to them openly (publicly), I never knew you; depart from me, you who act wickedly (disregarding My commands.)*
>
> Matthew 7:22&23

No matter how beautiful or attractive we are on the outside, if we do not have the life and light of God operating on the inside, we are nothing but decorated tombs.

No matter what we have achieved or acquired in life, if we do not have a yielded day-to-day relationship with God in our inner self, we are nothing but rotting dead bodies; then we have become so consumed with our fleshly desires that we cannot identify all the warning signals in our spirit that say we are dying spiritually. We prance around in our self-importance, ignorantly oblivious to the fact that we have gradually degenerated into dead bodies - living corpses. All that is left then is a form, mere religion.

> For (although) they hold a form of piety (true religion), they deny and reject and are strangers to the power of it (their conduct belies the genuineness of their profession). Avoid (all) such people (turn away from them).
>
> 2 Timothy 3:5

Chapter Eleven

AMIARA LANG

Amiara Lang, tall, dark, slim, beautiful... very beautiful 22 year old, had just arrived in town. This was her year of national service, one year of compulsory service to the nation after university.

She was quite excited to be out of her home state for the first time in her life. "This was going to be very exciting", she thought to herself. New place, new people, new culture, new language. Wow!

She had heard so many exciting, exhilarating things about National Service Year. This was the year of serious relationships and marriage proposals and so very many other interesting things. Oh! She just knew she would be having loads of fun.

Kosonki and Diamante her two closest friends were not as excited as she was. There was nothing about having your best friend from kindergarten flung 'to the ends of the ends of the earth' (so it seemed to them) for one whole year. What would they do without Amiara? She was the most intelligent, the most mature, the most creative of the three of them. Oh

God, life would be a bore without her.

For Amiara this was a very important stage of her life, she was not going to let anything get in her way. She had given much thought and planning to it all. After four years in University, then one year of national service during when she would meet her prince charming; within the next five years they should be married and done with child bearing, so she would concentrate on starting and running her own firm. She plans to be a very successful and very famous woman before she turns thirty-five.

The night before she left her beloved northern town of Valenbada, Amiara had checked and rechecked; everything was set and ready. She had enough provisions packed to last her until she gets a hang of the new place. She had had her presiding pastor write her a letter of introduction and recommendation to the headquarters of the "Perfect Everlasting Communion of Christ", a sister church of their church – "The Praise and Worship of Jesus Centre". As a leading member of the choir, she knew it would not be difficult at all to find a place for herself in the midst of brethren. Besides, her cousin's best friend was also a member of the Perfect Everlasting Communion of Christ and she was sure that was a good advantage.

Okay, so she had left the familiar sights of Valenbada and walked eagerly into the waiting embrace of the hilly city of Jokobikiti. She was sure this city would welcome her and be a place of great adventure and good fortune for her for the next one year or so.

* * *

Phew! No one had told her how exerting the physical training part of the programme would be. Very early mornings were not her thing, but what made it bearable was the praise and worship songs that her group, the Christian brethren sang out while the training went on. This morning it had been so motivating that she had joined in. In her usual gusto, her voice rang out strong and melodious even in the midst of the harmonious sounds of her new friends.

She chuckled to herself, "and who was that tall and handsome 'bearded tenor'"? "Bearded tenor" had stared at her from the moment she took her first note to the very end of the songs. It was when she thought her eye caught him walking toward her that she turned and quickly called out to her roommate to wait up for her as they both walked back to the room.

* * *

Two dinner parties in one night!! How on earth was she supposed to manage that?! There was the general Dinner and Dance organised for all the service members to close boot camp and there was the Dinner and Appreciation night organised by the Christian brethren.

The Christian brethren had the earlier time of 4pm- 7pm, while the Dinner and Dance was 8pm- 11pm. It was going to be a rollicking night. She had heard that it was at such nights that special relationships were initiated; when the guys took the bold steps of speaking up to the girls that they had had their eyes on, all camp long. Well, it would be interesting to see the kind of guys that had had their eyes on her, well except for "Bearded tenor" that is. "Teeheehee!" "What a great time to be alive!".

* * *

Perfect Everlasting Communion of Christ (PECOC) "Oh my God! What a blast!" The church was beyond her wildest dreams. It was like she was in heaven.

"What was that? Those lights! The music! The people! The choir! Oh the choir, what wouldn't she give to be a part of that glorious gathering of singing angels. Oh lord have mercy!"

She had almost screamed for joy when the presiding Bishop, Bishop Jakco said to her...

"From what Pastor Fredinko wrote about you, you would be an asset to our choir, welcome to church!"

"Yippee!!! Thank you Jesus!" She can't wait to tell Kosokin and Diamante the breathtaking news.

"And who was that she thought she saw in the choir? It couldn't have been or could it have? 'Bearded tenor'? No way!"

It was hilarious the expression on his face the other night. He had come over to her table at the Christian brethren's dinner party, and asked if he could take the empty seat beside her. She had shrugged nonchalantly and promptly turned her face away. He sat and had started to get familiar, she took one look at him, stood up, picked her bag and left the table. Immediately, his expression was like someone had wacked him hard across the face – "Teeheehee!" But now it wasn't so funny anymore. If "Bearded tenor" was a member of PECOC and a part of that prestigious choir, then she had fouled up real bad. "Oh God please help me." Amiara muttered under her breath.

* * *

Was everyone in the city of Jokobikiti a member of PECOC? That's three persons from her new office already, wasn't that something? Going to church on fellowship days from work was going to be a breeze. Two out of three had very comfortable cars so that took care of transport for her.

Her first choir rehearsal meeting was heavenly. Not to worry that all she got to do was sit and watch. The watching was all part of the rehearsal. It was like being with celebrities. Guess who was one of the biggest stars - 'Bearded tenor'. He turned out to be Head of Department - Music, wow! Funny though, it was like he did not even recognise her. Anyway, next time she would go up to him and say hi.

* * *

Anpere Bone, one of the consulting partners from the office was the head of PECOC's protocol team. That's the team closest to the Bishop himself. Upwardly mobile Anpere, was a very serious minded young man, bent on making it big in life and very committed to church. He did not mince words about his intentions towards her, and she considered him quite a catch too. It wasn't difficult to start to date him. The only problem was that 'Bearded tenor', oh sorry... Blake Isbanin; young and enterprising entrepreneur with a fast rising business (his suits where an obvious indication of how fast) who had started out as her music mentor, had now also become very insistent on taking the relationship to the next level. They had gone out on a few dates and she had found his passion and zeal to become a minister of God so strong almost overpowering. His mentor and role model was of course Bishop Jakco and his dream was to have a ministry and church just like PECOC.

How does one choose between two dashing and promising young men? Each one in his own way would compliment her dreams of establishing one of the biggest and best accounting firms in the country, and also give her the kind of life she desired and deserved. She knew she couldn't afford not to make the best choice from the two opportunities open to her. The two men were very close to Bishop Jakco – they were both aggressively ambitious, had very high standards, very good taste and were both unapologetically tenacious in their pursuit of power and success. It was quite obvious that both men would each in his own way turn out very successful.

Settling for anything less than men like these two was not in the cards for her. She was already a lead voice in the prestigious PECOC choir. Anytime she lifts up her voice in the congregation, the whole auditorium would vibrate in fascination, and thunderous applause would follow. Oh! God had really blessed her. To be truthful she knows she is quite a catch herself, Blake and Anpere should thank the Lord for the day they met her. They should both keep pressing for her hand and may the best man win. "Teeheehee!!!"

Chapter Twelve

FRIENDSHIP WITH GOD- OUR ONLY CALLING

Intimacy, is being involved with someone in a deep and personal way. Intimacy with God is deep sincere friendship with God. Intimacy with God is closeness with God. When we commune with God in deep, warm, relationship, we develop closeness with Him that is full of warmth and deep intimate feelings. We are embraced in His arms in close heart to heart relationship. We are linked in intense rapport and have a one on one connection with Him. Every other thing in life becomes insignificant when we are wrapped in God's warmth and presence. All we want is to conform to Him and His will.

Friendship is a covenant. A covenant is a relationship based on promises. This covenant relationship is designed to eliminate weak areas and give strength for destiny fulfilment. Friendship is designed to enhance our lives.

We need to be in a friendship relationship with God first, before we can succeed in any other relationship in life. The success of any relationship we will ever cultivate in life, depends on our relationship with God. Every other relationship in our lives take their life from our relationship with God. If the relationship we have with God is strained, dry, dull or practically non-existent, then our other relationships will be unsuccessful and un-fulfilling.

We cannot successfully relate with anyone except through God, the creator of all flesh. A fulfilling friendship relationship with God ensures that every other relationship in our lives fulfill their divine purpose. Friendship relationship with God is the key to our stability and prosperity in life.

When we have a friendship with God, we have a better understanding of the workings of the mind of God. Friendship with God gives us a clearer and deeper understanding of the works of God's hands, both physical and spiritual.

God reveals Himself and His ways and His creation to us in friendship. Abraham was in a friendship relationship with God. God Himself acknowledged Abraham as His friend.

But you Israel, My servant, Jacob, whom I have chosen, the offspring of Abraham My friend

Isaiah 41:8

By this friendship relationship between God and Abraham, God could not conceal Himself or His actions from Abraham. Friendship compelled God to divulge His plans of destroying

Sodom and Gomorrah to Abraham. Friendship compelled God to accept Abraham's plea to save Lot alive from Sodom and Gomorrah.

> *And the Lord said, Shall I hide from Abraham [My friend and servant] what i am going to do.*
> Genesis 18:17

> *When God spoiled and destroyed the cities of the plain [of Siddim], He [earnestly] remembered Abraham (imprinted, fixed him indelibly on His mind); and He sent Lot out of the midst of the overthrow, when He overthrew the cities where Lot lived.*
> Genesis 19:29

Moses also had a friendship walk with God. He was very intimate with God. They had heart to heart and mouth to mouth discussions. Moses could approach God's presence and commune with Him one on one. He had a deep walk with God.

When Miriam and Aaron criticized and spoke against Moses (Numbers 12), God rose up as advocate and judge on Moses' behalf. God told them in very clear terms that Moses was His friend, therefore no one was permitted under any circumstances to speak or to stand against him.

6. *And He said, Hear now My words: If there is a prophet among you, I the Lord make Myself known to him in a vision and speak to him in a dream.*

7. *But not so with my servant Moses; he is entrusted and faithful in all My house.*

8. *With him I speak mouth to mouth [directly], clearly and not in dark speeches; and he beholds the form of the Lord. Why then were you not afraid to speak against My servant Moses?*

9. *And the anger of the Lord was kindled against them, and He departed.*

Numbers 12:6-9

God defends His friends; He supports and sides with them. God stands up for His friends and fights for them. God empowers and strengthens His friends.

Iron sharpens Iron; so a man sharpens the countenance of his friend [to show rage or worthy purpose]

Proverbs 27: 17

A friend loves at all times,...

Proverbs 17:17a

...but there is a friend who sticks closer than a brother.

Proverbs 18:24b

Friendship with God is the key to triumphant and victorious living.

God is a God of relationships. God is all about relationships. He is relationship oriented.

God could have destroyed Adam and Eve completely without a trace when they sinned. He however chose not to. Why? Because He had already established a relationship with them.

8. *And they heard the sound of the Lord God walking in the garden in the cool of the day, and Adam and his wife hid themselves from the presence of the Lord God among the trees of the garden.*
9. *But the Lord God called to Adam and said to him, Where are you?*

Genesis 3:8-9

Even after they had sinned, relationship made God preserve them and cover them.

21. *For Adam also and for his wife the Lord God made long coats (tunics) of skins and clothed them.* Genesis 3:21

When the stench of sin was too much for God to bear, He came up against the earth, but He preserved out of the whole earth the man with whom He had a relationship - Noah.

This is the history of the generations of Noah. Noah was a just and righteous man, blameless in his [evil] generation; Noah walked [in habitual fellowship] with God.

Genesis 6:9

It was relationship that caused God to come down to earth to die and shed His blood.

12. *Giving thanks to the Father, who has qualified you to share in the inheritance of the saints in the kingdom of light.*
13. *For he has rescued us from the dominion of darkness and brought us into the kingdom of the Son he loves,*
14. *In whom we have redemption, the forgiveness of sins.*
15. *He is the image of the invisible God, the firstborn over all creation.*

16. *For by him all things were created: things in heaven and on earth, visible and invisible, whether thrones or powers or rulers or authorities; all things were created by him and for him.*

17. *He is before all things, and in him all things hold together.*

18. *And he is the head of the body, the church; he is the beginning and the first born from among the dead, so that in everything he might have the supremacy.*

19. *For God was pleased to have all his fullness dwell in him,*

20. *And through him to reconcile to himself all things, whether things on earth or things in heaven, by making peace through his blood, shed on the cross.*

21. *Once you were alienated from God and were enemies in your minds because of your evil behavior.*

22. *But now he has reconciled you by Christ's physical body through death to present you holy in his sight, without blemish and free from accusation.*

Colossians 1:12-22 NIV

The whole gospel is about relationship.

> 16. *And said, I have sworn by Myself, says the Lord, that since you have done this and have not withheld [from Me] or begrudged [given Me] your son, your only son,*
> 17. *In blessing I will bless you and in multiplying I will multiply your descendants like stars of the heavens and like the sand on the seashore. And your Seed (Heir) will possess the gate of His enemies.*
>
> Genesis 22:16-17

Abraham was committed to God in a friendship relationship. Abraham gave his only son to God as a sacrifice. God retaliated by giving His only Son for all mankind - through the friendship relationship commitment that He made with Abraham.

God values relationships. God's heartbeat is fellowship. It is all about relationship with God. God sacrifices for relationship. God puts Himself out for relationship. God is moved and provoked by relationship ties: "God of Abraham, God of Isaac and God of Jacob."

We are created for relationship. We are called to friendship. God is seeking us for friendship. God is calling out for friends. God is - for relationship. We are - for relationship. It is anti-God to be alone.

9. *Two are better than one, because they have a good [more satisfying] reward for their labor;*

10. *For if they fall, the one will lift up his fellow. But woe to him who is alone when he falls and has not another to lift him up!*

11. *Again, if two lie down together, then they have warmth; but how can one be warm alone?*

12. *And though a man might prevail against him who is alone, two will withstand him. A threefold cord is not quickly broken.*

Ecclesiastics 4:9-12

God typifies relationship in Him. God is relationship personified. He is, God the father, God the Son, God the Holy Ghost. God is also in fellowship with Himself. God is in relationship with Himself.

We are called to walk with God. Walking with God in close and in intimate fellowship signs and seals our destinies for prosperity. Walking with God is the essence of our existence.

When you have a close one-on-one intimacy with God, your whole life is affected. Relationship is in one word - INFLUENCE. You are definitely influenced by whoever you constantly and consistently relate with. Whoever you are in constant contact with greatly affects your life.

There is no way you relate with God intimately that you will not begin to take on His nature, His mentality, His personality, etc.

Your level of relationship with God determines your level of excellence in life. The closer you are to God, the more of His benefits you enjoy. We make God seem so far away from us because of the formal ways by which we relate to and with Him. God is calling us to closeness to Him.

The closer you are to God, the more access you have to all that belongs to God. Access comes from relationship and influence flows from intimacy. Your influence with God is in direct proportion to your level of intimacy with Him.

The more intimate you are with God, the more exposed you are to His power and invariably the more of His power you wield.

Instead of seeking prosperity, blessings and power we should seek God. Instead of hungering and craving for financial and material wealth, we should hunger and thirst for real wealth that is in sincere, intimate fellowship with God. Material, financial wealth can never satisfy us.

When we give God first place in our desires and in all our thoughts and ways, our thirst will be quenched, our hunger satisfied and satiated. We will have a deep fulfilment in our hearts and life.

When we study and quote scriptures without intimate fellowship with God in our inner lives, we can never have the life of these scriptures operate in our lives and circumstances.

Therefore we cannot live a life that is fulfilling or beneficial to us or to others.

Prayers and fasting without a close communion with the Holy Spirit will never produce the power of God. Occultists and Satanists also pray. They also fast for power.

There are no formulas to God's power. Only the Holy Spirit in our inner lives can produce in us the power of God.

No man can do ministry. Ministry is God's exclusive preserve. Ministry is God's work. God is the only one who can do ministry. All we can do and all we need do is be in habitual intimate fellowship with God and then He will do ministry through us.

The Bible says, "Enoch walked with God and he was not, for God took him"
Genesis 5:24

Enoch fulfilled destiny and there was nothing more to add, so God took him. He was a man who had a one on one relationship with God. He had a deep communion with God. They were always together. Always walking hand in hand, side by side, moving up and down together.

Enoch had the testimony that he pleased God. He held on tightly to God, believing and trusting in Him and not letting God out of his sight even for a second.

Because of the faith Enoch was caught up and transferred to heaven, so that he did not have a glimpse of death; and he was not found, because God had translated him. For even before he was taken to heaven, he receivedthe testimony [still on record] that he had pleased and been satisfactory to God.

Hebrews 11:5

Enoch's walk with God in intimacy and close companionship made him irresistible to God. God could not help but take him. Enoch was too close to God for God to leave him on the ordinary level. God just had to take Enoch up with Him to His own class, His own status. He had become a part and parcel of God.

Enoch's translation (i.e. his change, his improvement, his transformation from one level to the other, from the natural to the supernatural, from the ordinary to the extraordinary, to the exceptional, the remarkable,) came by his close companionship with God. Intimacy with God, broke for Enoch the protocol of death before resurrection.

Our calling, our SINGLE, most important calling is to walk with God - To walk with God in intimacy and in habitual close companionship. It is then that God will be able to work in us.

When we walk with God, He in turn now uses us to work for Him. He will do ministry through us. He will do the 'doing'.

When we do ministry, it is not God's ministry; it is our own ministry. We are the ones doing the ministry, so because of our doing, the ministry belongs to us.

It is God's ministry when we allow Him to "do" ministry through us. He can only use us and 'do" ministry through us when we give ourselves to Him in intimate fellowship.

Our business is to walk with God. Walking with God is all we are called to 'do'. That one thing we are saved, chosen and called unto Him for, is to walk with him. God's business is ministry. God is the one who DOES ministry, our business is walking with God. We 'do' walking with God.

Enoch's testimony was that all he did, he did to please God, not himself. He sought to please God in his life and with all his life. God came first. His walk with God opened his eyes of understanding to see that all he had to 'do' was please God. So he walked with God in intimacy and consistency and God now did ministry through him.

14. *It was of these people, moreover, that Enoch in the seventh [generation] from Adams prophesied when he said, Behold, the Lord comes with His myriads of holy ones (ten thousands of His saint)*

15. *To execute judgment upon all and to convict all the impious (unholy ones) of all their ungodly deeds which they have committed [in such an] ungodly [way], and of all the severe (abusive, jarring) things which ungodly sinners have spoken against Him.*

Jude 14&15

God used Enoch as a prophet, and the prophesies of God through him made relevant impact. Enoch was successful in ministry. In walking with God, Enoch fulfilled calling, he fulfilled ministry, for God did ministry through him the way He (God) wanted.

God is not far from us. God is near us. He wants to be our intimate friend. God is looking, seeking for people to call friends. He is going house to house, and heart to heart, calling for people who will go beyond the formality of religious worship and just fellowship with Him as a close, true friend.

"Look! Here I stand at the door and knock. If you hear me calling and open the door, I will come in, and we will share a meal as friends.

Revelation 3:20

Chapter Thirteen

DAMIEN DAPO DAVIES

Damien Dapo Davies was a self-made man. He had practically pulled himself up by his own bootstraps.

Friends and family had shut their doors in his face when he had solicited their helping hands.

His not too smooth hands and feet were a living reminder of his tough journey of crawling up the success ladder all by him. But hey! Here he was, and it felt good to be at the top. "Problem is, it sometimes got real lonely up here and somedays; everything just seemed absolutely meaningless".

Damien had just wrapped up another of his beautiful deals this evening and he was in a celebrating mood, considering also that it was his birthday; But whom with and how? Over the years he had not made any new close or intimate friends and he had walked away from his antagonistic, no-good, ill-meaning family. He had just been too busy and too wary to cultivate any personal relationships again, either male nor female.

So here he was, a 48 year old anti-social multi-millionaire, living in a huge 'castle' with housekeepers, cooks, stewards, maids, gardeners, drivers, dogs; but no wife, no children. Anyway, he was too set in his ways now to accommodate any female or little children into his life.

He would sit home tonight as usual and play a wonderful game of chess with himself. Damien switched on his computer in his den and at that moment his phone rang.

He did a quick mental rundown; did he forget to sign any papers on his desk? Did his General Manager have all the necessary documents for tomorrow's meeting? Was something wrong at one of the rigs? What could it be? He usually did not get night calls. Frowning, he picked up the phone.

"Hallo!" He answered.

"Hello Damien, this is Russel Vinodi." It was the CEO of Stylux Corp.

"Oh! Hi Russ!" Damien responded.

"Well, sorry to badge in on you like this buddy, but it's the American Ambassador's birthday and we just organized an impromptu, informal thing for him at my island for 10.00pm tonight. I was wondering if you would be gracious enough to join us. It's really a small thing; just the President, some Ministers and a few of us guys. It would be an honour to have you."

Damien's first thought was to make his excuses, but he hesitated for just a moment and thought, why not?

"Okay! Okay! How can I resist such a prestigious gathering," Damien answered. "Emm...its 9.40 already; let me just freshen up and I should be with you guys in about an hour or so. Is that alright?"

"Thank you for being such a sport; see you soon," Russel Vinodi gushed and rang off.

"Now what did I just do?" Damien muttered to himself. Anyway, he was sure it was his business brain ticking as usual. It could be very advantageous mingling with these decision makers and it was usually at informal gatherings like this that big and juicy things happened.

One hour twenty minutes later, Damien was mentally kicking himself. It was a mistake coming out here. He was bored stiff. After going through the preliminary introductions, slapping familiar backs and shaking some new hands, he found out there was so little that interested him here. The guys were bent on partying down tonight. No business deals or serious talk here, just empty banter and a lot of raucous laughter, edged on by a variety of exotic alcoholic drinks and the usual eager under-aged ladies.

He sat in a little corner all by himself, nursing his dealcoholised white wine, just watching the party. He was waiting for the right moment so he could slip away without much notice. He was almost yawning.

He lifted up his head from his drink to survey the place again and ...whoosh! He found himself staring into the most enthralling pair of eyes he had ever seen in his entire life. His world stood rock still in that instant. His breath just caught in his throat and he couldn't breathe. He suddenly got all light headed and giddy. "It must be the wine, it must be the wine," he thought wildly to himself, forgetting completely the wine was alcohol free.

"Beautiful eyes" moved towards him and Oh! No! He was sure he would pass out. Adrenaline flooded through him and he jumped to his feet. Crash! The glass he had been holding fell to the marble floor and shattered into pieces.

"This was not happening, Damien Dapo David? Cool, calm, collected and composed D.D.D? Unbelievable! Preposterous!" A waiter rushed up to him with cleaning equipment and started to apologize profusely like he was responsible for the mess. Damien, glad that that was taken care of, turned to see the object of his turmoil.

"Oh so sorry!" The words rolled out from her lips like silk on velvet. "I honestly thought you were someone else. Forgive me." With that, she turned right back and walked elegantly away from Damien.

Damien felt like his whole world had just fallen apart. He felt he would just slump and die. She had just walked away from him. Walk away from him! Never! He had to do something. He had to get her back. She had to know she had just made a mistake. He was the one she was looking for.

He knew she was the one he had been looking for all his life anyway. He had to go after her. Who is she?

Damien slept very little that night. By the time he got home he was mentally, physically and emotionally sapped. He had been a little embarrassed at first to ask Russel about the lady. But after searching for her with no success, he had given in and had casually enquired about the tall, slim, dark woman in the purple sequined gown.

Russel could not figure out who it was but he had made a promise to look seriously into the matter. He had been amused and very excited that D.D.D was showing any interest at all in something other than business and money.

Damien had thought by the morning light his brain would function clearer and normal. He just could not understand what had come over him. Now, after three cups of coffee, he was still trying very hard to shake the alluring image of those remarkable eyes out of his head.

Damien Davies did not play games. He now knew this was serious business. So he was not going to lie to himself and beat about the bush. He wants to know this person and get close to her. He had never in his life felt so strongly about anything, (well, anything outside making money) or anyone. He was going to do all he could to get introduced to this woman.

Just then his phone rang.

"Morning!" He said.

"A very good morning to you D.D.D," Russel's voice boomed. "Thank you so much for coming yesterday; I was really honored by your presence."

"Oh nothing to it buddy," said Damien, "It was all my pleasure."

"Well talking about pleasure," Russel continued, "I just got off the phone with my wife's cousin. Our mystery lady happens to be her friend and colleague she had brought along to the party. She is Miss Sherlin Saviour. She is the Chief Legal Officer for Malcox Group. I took the liberty of asking the two of them out to lunch today. I hope you don't mind. I have booked a table for us at the 'Four Seasons.'"

"Oh! wow!" Damien exhaled. "That's really good work Russ, and fast too, I must say. Well! It's okay by me. I am sure I can manage it. Thank you for all that trouble. So, guess I see you for 1:30 lunch time then?"

"Right!" said Russ as he hung up.

Damien rushed his coffee. He had to arrange for fresh flowers and chocolates. Nothing too showy, it was a first date. He checked his nails. He would get his nails done and also a haircut. He had to get his secretary to find out all she could about Miss Saviour, everything there is to know, her parents, her family, her schools, her favourite colour, food, everything.

He had just found a new vocation in life, a new passion. He had a strong feeling this passion was not going away, ever. He was ready to share Miss Saviour's life and he was more than ready for her to share his own. He would woo her and court her in all ways imaginable. He wanted her to feel his heartbeat and know his every thought. He would get into her head and into her heart. He would love Miss Saviour with everything he has and he was going to make sure that she loves him right back with the same intensity.

He was willing to make sacrifices for this woman. He wanted her to have his children, as many as she wants. He knew this was the person he had been waiting for all his life. Now his life will take up meaning. Up till now his life had been empty, this for him was the new beginning he had been unconsciously waiting for.

There would be nobody like her to him. He would make sure he was all in all to her. She would be the closest, most intimate person to him. He was ready for a deep relationship.

They would together take decisions. He would listen to her and inculcate her ideas. He was willing to be moulded by her. He would allow her break all the barriers he had erected around his heart all these years. Oh! Oh! 9:30, time to go!

Chapter Fourteen

MY FRIEND?

A friend is one joined to another in intimacy and affection (Oxford dictionary of Modern English).

Friendship is the greatest of all relationships. Friendship is deep communion. Friendship is transparent communication. Friendship is love and affection.

Friendship with God ENRICHES your life. Deep Communion with God in intimate friendship brings into your life and destiny, deposits of immeasurable value.

God is the Almighty God of all creation. He is the Great God of all being. The only true God, the only wise God. When we rub minds with Him in true sincere fellowship, our lives and destines take on great inexplicable value.

Friendship with God gives your life colour. Your life begins to mirror the multidimensional nature of God when you relate closely with Him.

In close friendship with God, the kaleidoscopic multifaceted beauty of God begins to reflect in your life and life's situations.

Intimate relationship with God gives your life meaning. It is not about what you have acquired, what you own, what title you have, or what you have accumulated.

Intimacy with God catapults you into the class of God. You are no longer an ordinary person. You become extra-ordinary. There is no way you relate with God intimately that you remain ordinary, no way!

When you are in friendship with God, God infuses into you His Nature, His abilities, His capabilities. As you walk steadily and conscientiously with Him in deep communion, you begin to think, speak and operate like God.

A good illustration of deep friendship communion with God is marriage between a man and a woman. In a solid marriage relationship, as the married couple continue to relate closely on a day-to-day basis with each other they become more intimately entwined.

They being to think alike, talk alike, gesticulate alike and even sometimes they begin to look alike. Their closeness and rubbing together in communion over time causes there to be an impartation of behavioral patterns, character and physical similarities between them.

This is exactly what happens when we relate deeply with God. Our relationship with God is described as a marriage. (Ephesians 5)

The same mystery of oneness between a married couple is the same mystery we engage in and enjoy when we join to God in intimacy.

We need to know who a close friend is. Here are some relevant points to help us understand who a close friend is:

One:

You cannot have a friend that you do not know his name; you must know the true identity of whoever you call friend. When you desire to be a friend of God, you must know who He is. You must know the true identity of the person of this God you want to have a close relationship with. You must be able to identify this God!

The Word of God says He is God the Father, God the Son, God the Holy Ghost. He is the trinity. God sent His only begotten son into the world to die and shed His blood for our sins and cleanse us from all iniquity.

Almighty God, in fulfilling His plan to redeem man whom He created in His image, took on human form in the person of Jesus Christ and came down to earth. Jesus Christ the Son of God, born of a virgin girl, died on the cross for all mankind and rose on the third day having conquered sin and satan. He sits on the right hand of God making intercessions for us.

He sent the Holy Ghost to us to comfort us, to teach us and to show us all things.

A friend of God must be clear about the true identity of God, so he knows exactly who he is relating with.

Two:

You cannot make friends with a person before being properly introduced.

A friend of God must be properly introduced to God. You meet this person you are planning on being friends with first. You meet on friendly terms.

> *But to as many as did receive and welcome Him, He gave the authority (power, privilege, right) to become the children of God, that is, to those who believe in (adhere to, trust in, and rely on) His name*
>
> John 1:12

> *For God so loved the world that He gave His only begotten Son, that whoever believes in Him should not perish but have everlasting life.*
>
> John 3:16 NKJV

The proper way to get acquainted with God is through salvation.

All flesh have sinned and come short of His Glory and all have made themselves enemies of God. By accepting the gift of salvation we are reconciled to God and we begin to cultivate friendship with Him.

> 12. *That at that time you were without Christ, being aliens from the commonwealth of Israel and strangers from the covenants of promise, having no hope and without God in the world.*
> 13. *But now in Christ Jesus you who once were far off have been brought near by the blood of Christ.*
> 14. *For He Himself is our peace, who has made both one, and has broken down the middle wall of separation,*
> 15. *Having abolished in His flesh the enmity, that is, the law of commandments contained in ordinances, so as to create in Himself one new man from the two, thus making peace,*
> 16. *And that He might reconcile them both to God in one body through the cross, thereby putting to death the enmity.*
> 17. *And He came and preached peace to you who were afar off and to those who were near.*
>
> Ephesians 2:12-17 NKJV

When you accept Jesus Christ as your personal Lord and Saviour, you have become introduced and acquainted with God.

Three:

You cannot have a friend that you know nothing about. When you get acquainted with a person you want to call friend, you then begin to get to know that person.

A friend of God must get to know the character and nature of God. Get God's autobiography, i.e. the word of God, and then begin to search the scriptures to get to know your friend.

> *You diligently study the Scriptures because you think that by them you possess eternal life. These are the Scriptures that testify about me.*
>
> John 5:39 NIV

The more of The Word of God you know, the more of God you know. Reading and studying The Word is by the help of the Holy Spirit. It is the Holy Spirit who gives understanding. So, let the Holy Spirit always be your guide and instructor when searching the scriptures.

A friend of God never outgrows the reading and studying of The Word. The more of The Word of God in your heart, the more of God you have in your spirit. When you have a close friend who is valuable to you, you never tire of knowing things about the person. You want to know more and more about your friend so that you can understand him more, all because this person means a lot of you. You want to get into your friends thoughts if possible. Reading and studying The Word of God is getting into God's thoughts.

Four:

You cannot have a close friend that you do not talk to constantly. You talk to your friend because you want your friend to know things about you. You want your friend to share your thoughts, your moments, your secrets, and your life.

The more value you place on your friend, the more of you, you want your friend to know. The closer your friend is to you, the more time you spend talking to your friend. Some friends spend hours talking to each other every day.

When you are God's friend you want Him to know all there is to know about you. You talk to God on a daily basis. You talk to God minute by minute, second by second. He is the friend that sticks closer than a brother;

He is always there beside you. If you are God's friend you will talk to Him all the time.

Friendship is companionship. Friendship is conviviality. You want to be together with your friend almost all the time. Friendship is togetherness, comradeship. A friend of God wants to be with God at all times. If you are a friend of God, you want to be in companionship with God. You want to be close to Him, not far from Him.

Apart from a set time of prayer to talk to God, you will make a conscious and constant effort to talk to God any time, every time, because He is your friend. You will want your communication with your friend to be more spontaneous. A friendship relationship with God transcends the formal level of religious prayer. You share your day with your intimate friend, your fears, your triumphs, your hopes, your aspirations, everything. There is nothing too small or too mundane to talk to your friend about. You want him to know everything as you also want to know all there is to know about your friend.

Communication is a two-way street. You do not only talk to your friend, you also listen to him. If you are always talking to your friend and never listening to him, you might soon lose a friend. You will also take time to listen to your friend because you care about your friend and about what he has to say. You know and recognize your friend's voice and you do not have a problem following your friend's counsel. You know your friend has your best interests at heart.

As a friend of God, you must listen to God. He is always talking and He is eager that we hear Him and follow His voice that we may triumph in life that we may prosper.

The sheep that are My own hear and are listening to My voice; and I know them, and they follow Me.

John 10:27

I [the Lord] will instruct you and teach you in the way you should go; I will counsel you with My eye upon you.

Psalms 32:8

Listening to God is very important to living as a Christian believer. It is by constantly hearing Him and following His leading, not the dictates of our heart and reasoning that we prosper abundantly. Many have stopped listening to Him so they don't hear Him. All they hear is their own reasoning.

Five:

When you desire a friendship relationship, you are willing to make sacrifices for that friendship.

Any friendship that is worth its salt has its sacrifices.

For example, when a young man is willing to make friends with a young maiden, he must be willing to make sacrifices to cultivate her friendship. The more valuable the maiden is to him the more sacrifices he is willing to make to be friends with her.

As a friend of God you must be willing to sacrifice your fleshly desires.

6. *Now the mind of the flesh [which is sense and reason without the Holy Spirit] is death [death that comprises all the miseries arising from sin, both here and hereafter]. But the mind of the [Holy] Spirit is life and [soul] peace [both now and forever].*
7. *[That is] because the mind of the flesh [with its carnal thought and purpose] is hostile to God, for it does not submit itself to God's Law; indeed it cannot.*
8. *So then those who are living the life of the flesh [catering to the appetites and impulses*

of their carnal nature] cannot please or
satisfy God, or be acceptable to Him.

Romans 8:6-8

As a friend of God, you cannot live after the dictates and desires of your fleshly nature. Friendship with God calls for a better standard. If you therefore desire sincerely to be God's friend, you will sacrifice your fleshly appetites. God sees those who follow after their fleshly desires as enemies not friends.

Six:

You do not want to set yourself against your friend. You want to please your friend as you want your friend to please you. No one desires to displease or fight with his friends. When you have an intimate friend, you value the relationship; you do not want it marred.

When you meet someone with whom you would like to be friends with, you want to know the person's likes and dislikes. You want to know the person's favorite things and things that put a smile on his face. You want to know because you want to do only the things that will please the person and make the person happy with you.

If you are friends with God, you will want to make God happy and do things that will endear you to Him. You will

116

want to obey God and do things that will put a smile on His face.

Doing the will of your friend is not a burden, it is no task. Obeying a friend is not an ordeal, it is a pleasure. When you are a friend of God, obeying God and doing His will is a pleasure not a pain.

Seven:

Friends are committed one to another. When you are in a friendship relationship with someone, you are committed to that person. You will look out for your friend. Your friend's concerns are yours. Your friend's burdens are yours. You can give your friend anything.

If you are friends with God, God's concerns automatically become yours. God's burdens become yours. You are committed to God and to the things of God. You can give to God anything and everything.

There is nothing too much or too little to give to your friend. As long as it is what is needful, you will give to Him because you are His friend and you are committed to Him in intimate friendship.

You will not hesitate to give of your substance to your friend, God. You evangelize and witness Christ at any and every given opportunity because this is God's heart cry.

You are zealous for God in all that you do because of the commitment of friendship.

Eight:

Your friend will influence you. There is no way you will not be influenced in a friendship relationship. Your friend will always rub off on you.

Friendship is in one word - INFLUENCE. Over time your friend will have an impact over your life.

The more you submit to your friend in love, the greater the influence your friend has over you.
Friends have been known to influence one another's decisions: in marriage, in business, in all areas of life.

When you submit to a friendship relationship with God, God will influence you. He will rub off on you. Apart from the fact that continuous constant intimacy with Him will produce in you a duplication of His nature, His thinking, His character, etc, He will also influence your decision making.

If before friendship with God you had done things in a certain way, because of friendship with Him, you will discover that you begin to do these same things in a different way. Your friendship with God influences your decisions in all matters of life. You are willing to be influenced in your decisions. You actually seek out this influence because of your friendship with Him. You want His friendship with you to be obvious to all your observers. You want them to see his influence over your life. You are proud to be friends with God and to be influenced by Him.

Nine:

Friendship is love. You love your friend. You care about your friend. You cannot have a friend you do not care about. Sincere friendship is love. Love is true. Love is faithful. Love is trust. Love is respect.

Friendship is sincerity. Friendship is transparency. You are sincere with and to your friend. Real friendship is not hypocritical. You are open with and to your true friend. Sincere friendship is perfect material for fulfillment and prosperity. God uses sincere friendship as a positive force for good things. Through sincere friendship, God brings us into His perfection.

Love is vital in true sincere friendship. A sincere friendship relationship is a covenant of love.

If you are friends with God, you will be faithful to Him; you will remain true to Him and you will trust and respect Him. You will stand firm and secure in your relationship with God, knowing that He is able to handle the affairs of your life.

You will remain calm and unruffled by life's circumstances, trusting in all that your friend has spoken concerning you, confident that your friend is able to do all that is within His power to give you the best.

You will always trust that your friend means you no harm or hurt; so whatever He tells you to do is for your good, and because He loves you, you will respect His counsel and opinion. You will also honour and respect His person.

Love is not selfish, love is not demanding, love is not self-centred. Love is not one-sided. When you are in a friendship relationship with God, it is not a one-sided thing. You love God for who He is. You are not in the relationship solely for what you will get but also for what you can give.

Ten:

Friends complement one another. Every friendship relationship is heading somewhere. Every friendship relationship is good for something. You will not continue to be friends with someone who is not adding positively to you.

If you are friends with God, you will make a positive impact in the kingdom of God. God does not have any useless friend. All God's friends are good for something. No one is useless before God.

In friendship relationship with God, you must have something positive that you are doing for God. As you make yourself available to Him, He will use you for one good thing or the other, as He pleases. Every friend of God is useful to God in the way that is pleasing to God.

Chapter Fifteen

OUTSTANDING PROSPERITY

Our walk with God is supposed to be progressive not retrogressive. We are supposed to move from one level of glory to another. Our inner and outer lives should reflect the light and life of God. God desires to make His dwelling place in us.

God works in us from the inside to the outside, so our inner life is of more interest to him. For it is what you have within that determines what you will be on the outside. It is what you have within that will also determine what you will bring out on the outside.

God wants us to live victorious, successful lives, but the way to prosperity and abundance is in intimate sincere consecration to God, not in religious activities or religious service. It is only by seeking God sincerely for who He is, not what he can give; that we can enter into His provisions.

If we sincerely and diligently seek God, we will know him in a deep intimate way. He will reveal Himself to us. If we determine to hear His voice and obey Him, He will make sure that He Himself satisfies us and we are not in need.

31. *Therefore do not worry and be anxious, saying, What are we going to have to eat? or, What are we going to have to drink? or, What are we going to have to wear?*

32. *For the Gentiles (heathen) wish for and crave and diligently seek all these things, and your heavenly Father knows well that you need them all.*

33 *But seek (aim at and strive after) first of all His kingdom and His righteousness (His way of doing and being right), and then all these things taken together will be given you besides.*

Matthew 6:31-33

The way to prosperity and abundance is in intimate fellowship with God. It is not in religion or spiritual methods and formulas. It is in habitual fellowship in our inner lives with the Holy Spirit. We need to get more into God than into ourselves.

On that great Day of Judgment, it is by the way we have lived our INNER LIVES that we will be judged. We will be judged by the substance of our hearts. The secret and deep things in our heart and minds will be made manifest and those things will be exposed to fire.

*On the day when, as my Gospel proclaims, God by
Jesus Christ will judge men in regards to the things
which they conceal (their hidden thoughts).*

Romans 2:16

Our innermost genuine motives for doing all the things we
did will be exposed and judged. We will not be judged
according to the number of church services we attended or
church activities we engaged in; not on the number of
churches or structures we built or did not build; not by the
miracles or signs or wonder that were wrought through us;
not by the titles we acquired, not by the projects we handled.
We will not be judged by the many crusades or revivals we
organized; not by the reputation we had with the church or
the world at large. We will not be judged based on our
affluence, our position, our fame or power.

22. *Many will say to me in that day, Lord, Lord,
have we not prophesied in thy name? and in
thy name have cast out devils? and in thy name
done many wonderful works?*
23. *And then will I profess unto them, I never
knew you: depart from me, ye that work
iniquity.*

Matthew 7:22-23 KJV

This will be the scene on that great Day of Judgment. Notice that Jesus did not deny that they truly did miracles, signs and wonders in His name. They did many mighty things by the name of Jesus not by any other name. They worked relentlessly in His name and by His power, yet He says to them, "depart from me, you WORKERS OF INIQUITY." This is terrible. They were working for God, but they were not walking with God.

This means the criteria for entering into the presence of God is not what most believe it is. We will not be judged based on what a lot of us assume.

We will be judged by what life we lived in our innermost selves. Our deepest thoughts and innermost longings will be the yardstick, the standard. Our secret lives and secret deeds will be the measure. Our character, our day-to-day thoughts will be the measure.

How do we live? What are the thoughts we think? What are the words we utter? How do we relate to, and with people?

* * *

The desire to be outward believers does not swoop on us in a day or at once. It is a gradual, step-by-step, day-by-day degeneration. One subtle trick here, one 'inconsequential' sin there, and before one knows it, the whole place is full of filth and the stench of hell.

We need to keep examining ourselves periodically. Are we still on the right track? Are we still living in PROGRESSIVE SANCTIFICATION? Have we started excusing the 'little sins'? Are our hearts still firmly fixed on pleasing God and God alone? Are we still willing to pursue God whether He gives us material blessings or not? Or is our service to God conditional? Service for blessings, no blessings no service?

> *Examine and test and evaluate your own selves to see whether you are holding to your faith and showing the proper fruits of it. Test and prove yourselves [not Christ]. Do you not yourself realize and know [thoroughly by an ever-increasing experience] that Jesus Christ is in you - unless you are [counterfeit] disapproved on trial and rejected?*
>
> 2 Corinthians 13:5

We need to critically scrutinize ourselves. Are we now living double lives, one secret filthy life, one public glowing life? Are we dead men on the inside, stinking rotten and foul smelling in our inner lives, but glowing and beautiful outwardly?

Our behavioral pattern is what we should closely examine. Do we have a penchant for lying, exaggerating and doctoring stories? How have our lives changed by the Christ Jesus we say we have received? Are we malicious? Do we have bad tempers? Are we full of envy? Do we backbite and gossip?

Are we arrogant and full of pride? Are we stubborn? Are we impatient? Are we covetous? These are questions we need to ask ourselves and answer truthfully and sincerely to determine the state of our inner selves.

Christianity is not about amassing riches and acquiring physical wealth. Christianity is about being transformed from the inside to the outside. Christianity is character.

Christianity is living a life of Christ, walking intimately day-by-day with Christ Jesus and being influenced by Him to become like Him. Ministry is not about fame, power, position and riches. Ministry is when you give yourself to God in obedience, so that your character can be transformed and through this affect your world positively.

As born-again believers, we are in the world but we are not of the world. This truth is not debatable; it does not have a best before date. It has not expired, neither is it out of fashion. WE ARE NOT OF THE WORLD.

We are just passing through here; we are on our way home. We have a better place that we belong to, a more permanent abode, a place that is home. We should not become too attached to this place and its comforts so much that we desire them more than our home comforts, that is, heavenly comforts. No matter how much we enjoy a foreign land or country, home is still where the heart is supposed to be. Our hearts are to pant after and fervently long for heavenly things (Spiritual things).

5. *For those who are according to the flesh and are controlled by its unholy desires set their minds on and pursue those things which gratify the flesh, but those who are according to the Spirit and are controlled by the desires of the Spirit set their minds on and seek those things which gratify the [Holy] Spirit.*

6. *Now the mind of the flesh [which is sense and reason without the Holy Spirit] is death [death that comprises all the miseries arising from sin, both here and hereafter]. But the mind of the [Holy] Spirit is life and [soul] peace [both now and forever].*

7. *[That is] because the mind of the flesh [with its carnal thoughts and purpose] is hostile to God, for it does not submit itself to God's Law; indeed it cannot.*

8. *So then those who are living the life of the flesh [catering to the appetites and impulses of their carnal nature] cannot please or satisfy God, or be acceptable to Him.*

Romans 8:5-8

Wealth, position and power should not become our reasons for living. These should not be our main concerns and pursuits in life. Success in life and ministry is not the reason we are here on earth. We are created to be used and manipulated by God. We are tools and instruments in His hands.

Material wealth is not wrong; financial and physical prosperity is not sin. God wants us to prosper and prosper abundantly too. God wants us to be outstandingly successful. He desires for us to excel, but living FOR OUR OWN PHYSICAL GRATIFICATION IS NOT the success God planned for us.

> Beloved, I pray that you may prosper in every way and [that your body] may keep well, even as [I know] your soul keeps well and prospers.
>
> 3 John 2

God desires that our SOUL prospers FIRST. This is His main, primary, concern - the prosperity of our inner man. God has given us gifts, abilities, strengths, that He wants to use in HIS OWN WAY for HIS OWN pleasure and HIS OWN GLORY.

When we focus on our needs and wants, our blessings and breakthroughs, we cannot be the success God wants us to be.

Coming to God and giving our lives to Him as born-again believers is no guarantee that we will live in affluence and opulence. He did not guarantee that by giving our lives to Him we would live here without challenges.

The fact that we give our lives to God, read the bible, fast frequently, speak with other tongues, pay the Lord's tithe, give good offerings, etc., does not automatically translate us into unimaginable riches. Christianity is not a formula for riches and material success. Christianity is walking with God to achieve God's plan and God's purpose.

> *I have told you these things, so that in Me you may have [perfect] peace and confidence. In the world you have tribulation and trials and distress and frustration; but be of good cheer [take courage; be confident, certain, undaunted]! For I have overcome the world. [I have deprived it of power to harm you and have conquered if for you.]*
>
> John 16:33

We are guaranteed peace when our whole hearts and minds are fixed on God; we will have peace in our inner lives, in our inner being. The outside world and its effects might be tumultuous but we will have peace in our inner selves. Close communion with God generates peace in our inner lives.

> *You will guard him and keep him in perfect and constant peace whose mind [both its inclination and its character] is stayed on You, because he commits himself to You, leans on You, and hopes confidently in You.*
>
> Isaiah 26:3

Knowing God intimately and focusing on Him in our inner lives is what gives us extraordinary achievements.

The secret of strength, the secret of extraordinary accomplishments and great outstanding achievements, is locked up in KNOWING GOD.

> ...*but the people who know their God shall prove themselves strong and shall stand firm and do exploits [for God].*
>
> Daniel 11:32b

Paul in Phillipians 3:10-14 puts it so succinctly. Verse 10 says, "that I may know Him..." That is, I have dedicated myself to seek Him out; I have separated myself to sift out viable information about Him; to find out truth about Him; I have only one mission in life, only one goal and that is to know Him. I consider every other thing in life as inconsequential, insignificant. Only one thing is important to me, to become deeply acquainted with Him and to intimately relate to Him.

There is 'excellency' in knowing God. The 'NIV' refers to it as 'Surpassing greatness'; the 'AMP' calls it 'overwhelming preciousness and supreme advantage'.

Knowing God is more than reading, studying and quoting scriptures. The Scribes, Pharisees and Sadducees were experts in the scriptures of their day. There was virtually nothing they did not know about the Book of the Law and the

Words of the prophets. But when Jesus stood before them, they could not recognize Him as God.

Demons would scream and shout, "We know you, 'Jesus the son of the Most High God.'" But Jesus' own people failed to recognize Him. They knew the scriptures, they could quote it word for word, letter for letter, they could manipulate it here and there, they could preach it from dawn to dusk, but they did not KNOW God.

They were full of information and knowledge, but they did not possess the Life of God.

> *You diligently study the Scriptures because you think that by them you possess eternal life. These are the Scriptures that testify about me.*
>
> John 5:39 NIV

The knowledge of the scriptures without the life of God on the inside of us is just dead letters and head knowledge. The knowledge we have of God, must lead us to God.

Knowing God on our inside is acknowledging God in all that we think, in all that we say and in all that we do. God must be our standard, our yardstick. We must always consider Him in our reactions. "What would God have me say?" "What would He have me do?" "How would He have me react to this?" This is having God deep inside us and having Him reflect out to our outward life. Our submission and complete compliance to God is what moulds our character to become what it should be.

* * *

We are no different from the world when we live and think only of our needs and wants. We are called to Christ to stand out, to be different. We are to live in life as examples for others of the world to see, to copy, to follow. When all our physical and spiritual energies and exercises are focused on our provisions, our supplies, our desires, we cannot have the outstanding achievements God has in store for us. As Christians we should focus on God and we should stop being self-centred and physically minded.

1. *If THEN you have been raised with Christ [to a new life, thus sharing His resurrection from the dead], aim at and seek the [rich, eternal treasures] that are above where, Christ is, seated at the right hand of God.*
2. *And set your minds and keep them set on what is above (the higher things), not on the things that are on the earth.*

Colossian 3:1-2

When we are focused on God, filth and death cannot remain in us. The more we abide in Him, the more He works to purge us of all defilement, of all corruption.

Even when we falter and fall, when we go wrong and we start to stink, there is hope for us. Because of His love for us and by our relationship, He points out to us our faults, our failings and mistakes. He works in us to pick us up, wash us clean and establish His life on the inside of us. He will bring us to that point of repentance and He will deliver us.

> 9. *If we [freely] admit that we have sinned and confess our sins, He is faithful and just (true to His own nature and promises) and will forgive our sins [dismiss our awlessness] and [continuously] cleanse us from all unrighteousness [everything not in conformity to His will in purpose, thought, and action].*
>
> 1 John 1:9

> 4. *Then I said, I have been cast out of Your presence and Your sight; yet I will look again toward Your holy temple.* [Psalms 31:22].

> 5. *The waters compassed me about, even to [the extinction of] life; the abyss surrounded me, the seaweed was wrapped about my head.*
>
> [Psalms 69:1; Lamentations 3:54.]

6. *I went down to the bottoms and the very roots of the mountains; the earth with its bars closed behind me forever. Yet You have brought up my life from the pit and corruption, O Lord my God.*

7. *When my soul fainted upon me [crushing me], I earnestly and seriously remembered the Lord; and my prayer came to You, into Your holy temple.*

Jonah 2:10

10. *And the Lord spoke to the fish, and it vomited out Jonah upon the dry land.*

Jonah 2:4-7,10

As we walk steadfastly with Him, our minds will be renewed to conform to Him. As we spend quality time with Him, we take on His image. When we are fully committed to His will and walk by His word in true, sincere consecration and communion, He will direct us in His own way to the successes that are truly ours and we will be content and fulfilled in them.

The key to successful living is what and who we are focused on. When we are completely focused on God, He will help us by the Holy Spirit, to begin to think His thoughts. We will begin to live His mind and manifest His life.

22. *But the fruit of the [Holy] Spirit [the work which His presence within accomplishes] is love, joy (gladness), peace, patience (an even temper, forbearance), kindness, goodness (benevolence), faithfulness,*

23. *Gentleness (meekness, humility), self-control (self-restraint, continence). Against such things there is no law [that can bring a charge].*

Galatians 5:22-23

Chapter Sixteen

PELIANA DUNCAN

Peliana Duncan, a young woman of contrasts. Small, light, but athletic and strong. Very smart, very serious but she also possessed a magnetic sense of humour; a lovely girl, a great future.

She had had a tough life; familiar heart-rending story - father left mother with a big blown out stomach on the church steps. After that, life had been a myriad of aches, disillusionment, disappointment, drugs and all what not.

Growing up, Peliana's sense of humour had kept her sane and she had kept hitting back at life with all she had. When her mother finally died of an overdose, she gave in to pressure and knuckled under. She met Christ at the "rehab" and she had opened the salvation package cautiously and suspiciously.

She was a fast learner though, and before long she had discovered a new lease of life. What she kept telling people that she enjoyed the most was the "peace and inexplicable joy" she experienced as she walked with God a step at a time, a day at a time.

When Peliana left the rehabilitation centre five and a half years ago, she had found a job at the counter of a local drug store. She had enrolled in night school so she could take her ordinary level papers. It had taken a lot of hard work, persistence, tears, sometimes outright balking. Her pastor and his wife had been so supportive. They had given her the best any young girl could ever ask for... And now she was geared to study Pharmacy at the prestigious "City University." It had been a long haul.

"Let's go, let's go, I can't wait to get home," Peliana mumbled as they walked out from the store.

"What's the hurry?" asked Betty Torra, packing the groceries into the trunk of the car.

"I just need to get home," Peliana responded. Peliana felt burdened and uneasy tonight, she needed to be alone with God. Since she received the admission letter this morning she had been so troubled in her spirit.

Peliana was already half way into the house by the time the car door slammed shut. Pastor Woffery Torra exchanged glances with his wife.

"What's biting her tonight?" He asked as they carried stuff into the house. Betty shrugged.

Peliana spent more than two hours locked up in her room. Strains from Marvin Sapp's worship tape could be heard coming from the room. By the time she got out, her eyes were sparkling and her face had a glow. She went straight into Pastor Woffery's study.

"Now I know..." she said softly, kneeling at Pastor's feet. Betty was sitting beside her husband doing crosswords.

"Know what dear?" Betty asked, looking up from her book.

"I know now what God wants me to do... I can't go to the University." Peliana gushed, "I can't marry Gray Park... and God has shown me that He wants me to train at the local study centre as a translator to be a missionary to the Far East... I know this is so far out from your plans for me, but I feel Him so strongly... Oh! I am so sorry!" she finished in a rush.

Pastor Woffery and Betty Torra were completely speechless.

When Woffery Torra finally got himself together, he managed to ask weakly,

"So, Peliana, when did you get this fascinating revelation?" Peliana stood up, and started walking up and down, talking rapidly and gesticulating wildly.

"Well I had been feeling uncomfortable for weeks now and I couldn't quite place it. I had been having these dreams and visions. So I started spending more time alone with God. However, this afternoon... " She paused, stopped moving, took a deep breath, and then continued gently. "I was worshipping and listening for His voice when He spoke to me expressly." She finished softly.

A spark flared in Pastor Betty Torra's eyes, unmistakable anger was there.

"Gary Park is the most eligible bachelor in church! He is rich! He is serious minded! He is the head of the Counseling Unit! After all we have done for you; you choose to ridicule us this way? What would you have people say?" Betty shrieked.

"Oh, but I think maybe we could pray over this together and seek Him on what He wants," Peliana pleaded.

"Hogwash! Absolute cow dung!" Betty snapped to her feet.

"Please watch your language dear," interjected Woffery in a frayed voice.

"Oh! Peleese!" Betty snarled as she made for the door. "I would not watch this ungrateful little wretch rub us in grime. God is not a fool! He would never dip so low and ask such a dingbat thing. He knows our class and status and He would not drag us in mire." Betty stalked out of the room. Halfway through the door she turned around, looked back at her husband and pointing at Peliana, she thundered ...

"It's absolutely preposterous what she is proposing and I would never consent to it. It's either the University and Gary or the University and Gary, no alternatives!!!" With that she turned and slammed the door shut with a loud bang.

Chapter Seventeen

A Definite Pattern
For Each Life

Seeking intimacy and desiring a close walk with God is not sitting still and folding our arms in laziness and slothfulness. Seeking intimacy with God is in itself disciplined hard work. Seeking intimacy with God opens the eyes of our understanding to know the will of God for our lives.

In intimacy and close companionship with God, we get a very clear picture of the course of our life. As we walk with Him closely and commune with Him intimately, God reveals to us the right way to go. He gives us direction in life by His word.

> *You will show me the path of life; in Your presence is fullness of joy, at Your right hand there are pleasures forever more.*
>
> Psalms 16:11

Walking with God is walking on the path that leads to success and fulfillment. We walk with Him by His Word. We believe in His Word, meditate daily on it and live in obedience to it.

> I [the Lord] will instruct you and teach you in the way you should go; I will counsel you with My eye upon you.
>
> Psalms 32:8

Intimacy with God ensures that we do not walk amiss. Close communion with God ascertains that we do not go round and round in confusing circles without making any profitable or significant progress in life and in ministry. When we talk to Him in close communion, we also listen to Him. We know His voice, we recognise His leading. We do not make or take decisions without His consent.

When we are in close companionship with God, we will know His will and purpose for our lives. As we get more into His Word, we will not flounder in the dark. We will gain speed and make meaningful impact. Our lives will impart others positively, therefore making us relevant in our world.

Our time here on earth should be used in service to God, not in pursuit of our own desires and plans. We are to live in the world but not become overtaken or obsessed by the provisions and comforts of the world.

15. *Do not love or cherish the world or the things that are in the world. If anyone loves the world, love for the Father is not in him.*

16. *For all that is in the world - the lust of the flesh [craving for sensual gratification] and lust of the eyes [greedy longings of the mind] and the pride of life [assurance in one's own resources or in the stability of earthly things] - these do not come from the Father but are from the world [itself].*

17. *And the world passes away and disappears, and with it the forbidden cravings (the passionate desires, the lust) of it; but he who does the will of God and carries out His purposes in his life abides (remains) forever.*

1 John 2:15-17

When we are truly intimate with God, He will work in us to genuinely lift others. He will give us and others through us, testimonies that are life transforming and permanent. He will give us testimonies that will reverberate through time. The awesome power of God will be made manifest in our lives and lives situations for others to see. This is outstanding success.

A big and prosperous ministry is not wrong. Big church structures and extensive and colossal projects might not be wrong. Big crusades and mammoth revivals are not sin.

Affluence, fame and power are not evil. We should seek God, His will, His desire, His plan and His purpose. If He chooses to do big, awesome ministry and build mighty, gigantic structures through us, that then is HIS PLAN. We should seek HIS PLAN not ours. We should follow HIS blue print not ours.

There are big, visibly prosperous ministries that are of God and from the mind of God. There are ministers of the gospel that God Himself has given fame, affluence and power. They followed HIS PLAN for them and they prospered thereby. These ministries and ministers need no formula or gimmicks. God Himself has decreed His display of prosperity, His wealth, His fame and His power over them. These ministers and ministries have His full backing and are under His profound covering. We need to know and follow GOD'S PLAN for us not our own self-motivated agendas.

When we do not use the gospel for our own self-actualization, but we let God use us for His purposes; this is success. When we are totally, completely filled with God and we manifest and reveal the life and light of God wherever we go, in whatever we do, either in secret or in the open; this is prosperity.

When we focus on God and exude His peace and His power. When we live by His standards, when we radiate His beauty and His love; This is excellence.

When we surrender completely to Him, conforming our will to His will and following Him gladly wherever He leads, under any and in every condition; doing as He pleases, this then is success in life and in ministry.

Every individual in Christ has an assignment. We have all been called as builders in one way or the other.

> 8. *He who plants and he who waters are equal (one in aim, of the same importance and esteem), yet each shall receive his own reward (wages), according to his own labor.*
> 9. *For we are fellow workmen (joint promoters, laborers together) with and for God; you are God's garden and vineyard and field under cultivation, [you are] God's building.*
> 10. *According to the grace (the special endowment for my task) of God bestowed on me, like a skillful architect and master builder I laid [the] foundation, and now another [man] is building upon it. But each [man] be careful how he builds upon it.*
>
> 1 Corinthians 3:8-10

Not every born again believer is called to the pulpit, but we are all called in one area of life or the other. Our assignments are the core reasons for our living as Christians. When we fail to enter into our assignments, our lives have no significance, no merit, no value, and no use. This is why we must desire to diligently seek God to know and enter into His plan and purpose for our lives.

Every profession is an assignment. We are assigned into different professions. We are all called to proclaim and glorify God in whichever profession or area of life we may find ourselves. God has planned and mapped out our lives so that we may speak for Him wherever and in whatever He has called us to do.

When we are not doing what we are supposed to be doing, the devil always finds for us something else to do. This substitute or alternate assignment is always the distraction that works to destroy our lives and destinies.

1. *In the spring when kings go forth to battle, David sent Joab with his servants and all Israel, and they ravaged the Ammonites [country] and besieged Rabbah. But David remained in Jerusalem.*

2. *One evening David arose from his couch and was walking on the roof of the king's house, when from there he saw a woman bathing; and she was very lovely to behold.*

3. *David sent and inquired about the woman. One said, Is not this Bathsheba, the daughter of Eliam and the wife of Uriah the Hittite?*

4. *And David sent messengers and took her. And she came in to him, and he lay with her - for she was purified from her uncleanness. Then she returned to her house.*

5.   *And the woman became pregnant and sent and told David, I am with child.*

                              2 Samuel 11:1-5

David's assignment at that time was on the battlefield, but he was not engaged in this God-given assignment, so invariably he was given a substitute assignment. That one singular act of adultery led him further to acts of trickery, deception, cunningness, and eventually to murder.

6.   *David sent to Joab, saying, Send me Uriah the Hittite. So Joab sent [him] Uriah.*

7.   *When Uriah had come to him, David asked him how Joab was, how the people fared, and how the war progressed.*

8.   *David said to Uriah, Go down to your house and wash your feet. Uriah went out of the king's house, and there followed him a mess of food [a gift] from the king.*

9.   *But Uriah slept at the door of the king's house with all the servants of his lord and did not go down to his house.*

10. *When they told David, Uriah did not go down to his house, David said to Uriah, Have you not come from a journey? Why did you not go down to your house?*

11. *Uriah said to David, The ark and Israel and Judah live in tents, and my lord Joab and the servants of my lord are camping in the open field. Shall I then go to my house to eat and drink and lie with my wife? As you live and as my soul lives, I will not do this thing.*

12. *And David said to Uriah, Remain here today also, and tomorrow I will let you depart. So Uriah remained in Jerusalem that day and the next.*

13. *David invited him, and he ate with him and drank, so that he made him drunk; but that night he went out to lie on his bed with the servants of his lord and did not go down to his house.*

14. *In the morning David wrote a letter to Joab and sent it with Uriah*

15. *And he wrote in the letter, Put Uriah in the front line of the heaviest fighting and withdraw from him, that he may be struck down and die.*

16. *So when Joab was besieging the city, he assigned Uriah opposite where he knew the enemy's most vigilant men were.*

17. *And the men of the city came out and fought with Joab, and some of the servants of David fell. Uriah the Hittite died also.*

2 Samuel 11:6-17

All these brought upon David and indeed his household a myriad of woes and tribulations.

> 10. *Now, therefore, the sword shall never depart from your house, because [you have not only despised My command, but] you have despised Me and have taken the wife of Uriah the Hittite to be your wife.*
>
> 11. *Thus says the Lord, Behold, I will raise up evil against you out of your own house; and I will take your wives before your eyes and give them to your neighbor, and he shall lie with your wives in the sight of this sun.*
>
> 12. *For you did it secretly, but I will do this thing before all Israel and before the sun.*
>
> 2 Samuel 12:10-12

David's reign was full of wars and bloodshed. His life was a tale of deceptions, sorrow, tears, heartbreak, insurrection, incest, exile and so on. His sons rose against him at different times. One slept with David's wives in full view of the whole nation; one committed incest with his sister (David's daughter). It was one sad story after another. All because he left his God-given assignment field and accepted an alternate assignment of misdemeanour and shame.

We need to find out God's plan and purpose for us par time, for our lives and destines. This is when we can move beyond merely existing and then really start to live.

Our God given assignments in life give our lives meaning and value. Our assignment confirms to us and to others that we are not worthless. Our assignment is the ministry God wants to do through our lives and this works in us to generate joy and fulfillment.

We are here on a mission. We are all pilgrims and sojourners here on earth.

> *Beloved, I implore you as aliens and strangers and exiles [in this world] to abstain from the sensual urges (the evil desires, the passions of the flesh, your lower nature) that wage war against the soul.*
>
> 1 Peter 2:11a

As children of God we are here on duty. There is a definite particular purpose for our being here on earth. We are not here by chance. We are not here by happenstance. We are ambassadors from Christ Jesus. We are sent out from Him on a mission.

> *So we are Christ's ambassadors, God making His appeal as it were through us. We [as Christ's personal representatives] beg you for His sake to lay*

hold of the divine favor [now offered you] and be reconciled to God.

2 Corinthians 5:20

But we are citizens of the state (commonwealth, homeland) which is in heaven,…

Philippians 3:20a

We are all positioned here on earth as workers of Christ. The Bible says we are commissioned soldiers on duty.

Take [with me] your share of the hardships and suffering [which you are called to endure] as a good (first class) soldier of Christ Jesus.

2 Timothy 2:3

We have been posted out here on only one main mission.

19. *Go then and make disciples of all the nations, baptizing them into the name of the Father and of the Son and of the Holy Spirit,*
20. *Teaching them to observe everything that I have commanded you, and behold, I am with you all the days (perpetually, uniformly, and on every occasion), to the [very] close and consummation of the age. Amen (so let it be).*

Matthew 28:19-20

And He said to them, Go into all the world and preach and publish openly the good news (the Gospel) to every creature [of the whole human race].

Mark 16:15

As believers of Christ Jesus, we have all been commissioned to evangelize the world in the name of Christ Jesus. We all have one mission. We all have the full backing and full support of heaven on that one mission.

There is ONE MISSION for every believer and follower of the Lord Jesus Christ and that is to spread the good news of the birth, crucifixion, death and resurrection to glory of our Lord and Saviour and to make disciples for Him.

Each individual has a specific, definite peculiar assignment here on earth. Even though we are all on one main mission, we are each on SEPARATE ASSIGNMENTS.

5. *There are different kinds of service, but the same Lord.*
6. *There are different kinds of working, but the same God works all of them in all men*
12. *The body is a unit, though it is made up of many parts, and though all its parts are many, they form one body. So it is with Christ.*

18. *But in fact God has arranged the parts in the body, every one of them, just as he wanted them to be.*
20. *As it is, there are many parts, but one body.*
27. *Now you are the body of Christ, and each one of you is a part of it.*

1 Corinthians 12:5,6,12,18,20,27 NIV

We have been equipped prior to this time for our separate, specific assignments. All we need do is for each of us to find out our specific assignments, stay with it and work at it diligently. We are not on earth just to eat and sleep. We are not here to while away time. We are here on specific detailed duty.

We should not look into others assignment fields in envy and covetousness, but focus on our own work portion diligently and conscientiously, in singleness of heart, attitude and in sincerity.

Let every man abide in the same calling wherein he was called.

1 Corinthians 7:20 KJV

Let us imagine two individual ambassadors from the same home government, each to a different, separate, nation. Their home government would equip the two for their assignment fields, but the peculiarities of their assigned nation would classify their 'provisions'. The ambassadorial mission is the same - to represent the home government; to please and seek the interest of the home government and to project and protect the image of the home government.

One as an ambassador to a developing nation in the tropics and the other as an ambassador to a developed nation bordering the arctic ocean; two ambassadors from the same home government to two different climate regions. These two ambassadors will have more than adequate provisions for their assignments. The home government will do its utmost to equip them properly, but the peculiarities of these two separate nations where they have been sent will characterize and dictate the provisions that would be made for each ambassador. An ambassador to a nation in the tropics will not be equipped with the same provisions as an ambassador to a nation in the arctic. The provisions for an ambassador to a developed nation cannot be the same for an ambassador to a developing nation.

The weather, politics, economy and social climate of each nation will play a major role in dictating the provisions made and given to each ambassador.

It will be foolhardy and unreasonable for the two ambassadors to expect the same provisions and equipping. They both will be thoroughly furnished; their home government will make sure they lack nothing. For no ambassador lives and works in lack.

They will have equal provisions. Equal, meaning equivalent, meaning corresponding; but they will definitely not have the same provisions. Their provisions will be equal in ambassadorial value, but not the same in specifics. Their assigned nations are distinctly different.

Though they are both commissioned and sent forth by the same home government on the same basic mission, they each have two very distinct assignment fields. Invariably they will have two distinct living patterns on their assignment fields.

When each ambassador has a good and clear understanding of his assignment and his assignment field, when each understands the peculiarities and distinct features of his work, they will not expect to have the same provisions. Therefore each will accept his allocated provision without contention. Knowing they have been given the best for the work ahead, they will go on their assignments gladly with singleness of heart and purpose to work diligently to succeed in their given fields.

God's plan and purpose for each individual is different. God operates the same principles for us all as born again believers, but He has different patterns for each one of us as separate individuals. It is God who determines the peculiarities and the standards, based on what He has planned for each person.

The way God is working in Mr A's life, is not the same way He is working in Mr Q's life. The way He will do ministry

155

through Apostle P might not be the same way He will do ministry by Apostle G.

It would be ignorance and foolishness to try to set the pattern of our lives according to someone else's life pattern. We are all cut and called different. We are on different assignments. Our assignments dictate and determine our lives. God has different patterns for each individual.

We need to know, understand, and stay with our own peculiar pattern and in our own assignment and calling. This is where our success, prosperity and fulfillment lie. We cannot all live and work and look the same, but we can all be fulfilled if we learn God's peculiar pattern for our individual lives and work with it to God's expected end.

Chapter Eighteen

God Desires That We Prosper

Τrue riches, true wealth is neither material nor physical. True wealth is not worldly - it is not earthly. True riches is, in knowing Christ Jesus intimately.

Success and prosperity is in fulfilling the plan and purpose of God for our lives. A successful man is a man who has been able to find God's plan and purpose for his life and has followed through with it.

A man who has spent his whole life chasing after material wealth and physical success, even though he is rich in worldly goods and possessions, if he has not been able to know and follow through in the plan and purpose of God for his life, is nothing but a complete failure and a waste.

Prosperity is, knowing God in your inner life and being able to affect your world positively with that knowledge of God. Prosperity is imparting others with the life and love of God. A man who has money, fame and power in this world, but has not been of any use or value to the people around him is a poverty stricken man. This kind of man is living in abject poverty.

Religion is not godliness. A man who has perfected the art of religion is not a godly or righteous man. He is a religious man. TheHi nowledge of God is from the heart, not from the head. "Outward forms of Christianity" is mere religion; which is, going through the motions but not applying the heart in sincerity. When such a 'Christian' wields power, he wields religious power. All he has is an appearance, an arrangement. The living fire and power of God is absent on the inside of that man.

They will act as if they are religious, but they will reject the power that could make them godly. You must stay away from people like that.

2 Timothy 3:5 NLT

Money, knowledge, acquisitions, position, and so on have power of their own. A rich, knowledgeable, highly placed man who has achieved much in the world is naturally a person of power. This however does not make him a righteous or godly man. This man wields power. Only that his power is worldly, temporal and transient.

True lasting power is from the Presence of God. Real power is the life of God Himself. Wherever God is, there His power manifests. Where God cannot abide, His power can never be present there. God is holy, He cannot abide with filth, and His eyes cannot even behold sin. A life that has sin, filth and rot stored within it cannot house God and can never manifest God's power. God's power is unadulterated and eternal. It does not fade, it does not die.

A man who carries within him the presence of God will manifest the awesome power of the living God. Wherever this man is, the power of God is present there. A man whose heart is clean and pure in God, whose private life is righteous in God, this man will manifest God's power.

God is too big to be concealed. Where God is, He announces Himself. When you have God with you, and on the inside of you, He will announce His presence in you to the outside world. He announced Himself in little David, the Shepherd boy (1 Samuel 17). He announced Himself in the home of Obed-Edom (2 Samuel 6:11). He proclaimed Himself in obscure, inconsequential Gideon (Judges 6). He announced Himself in Mary, the little virgin girl (Matthew 1). He announced Himself in the wilderness in the midst of the Israelites (Joshua 9:9).

When God is present and resident in a man's life, that man needs no gimmicks, strategies or stunts to get him into the limelight, God Himself will do the publicity and the proclamation - this is fame.

10. *When they came to the hill [Gibeah], behold, a band of prophets met him; and the Spirit of God*

came mightily upon him, and he spoke under divine inspiration among them.

11. *And when all who knew Saul before saw that he spoke by inspiration among the [schooled] prophets, the people said one to another, What has come over [him, who is nobody but] the son of Kish? Is Saul also among the prophets?*

12. *One from that same place answered, But who is the father of the others? So it became a proverb, Is Saul also among the prophets?*

13. *When [Saul] had ended his inspired speaking, he went to the high place.*

1 Samuel 10:10-13

Where God is not present, diverse aggressive publicity strategies and methods will be employed. The whole world may commend such a man, but this man may remain nameless and unheard of to God.

22. *Many will say to Me on that day, Lord, Lord, have we not prophesized in Your name and driven out demons in Your name and done many mighty works in Your name?*

23. *And then I will say to them openly (publicly), I never knew you; depart from Me, you who act wickedly [disregarding My commands]*

Matthew 7:22-23

True prosperity, true success, real power, profound wealth and unsearchable riches with unimaginable fame come from being acquainted with God. When you really know God, you will be exposed to riches in your innermost. Your soul will flow with ever increasing wealth and treasures unimaginable. Acquaintance with God is the secret of everlasting riches.

21. *"Now acquaint yourself with Him, and be at peace; thereby good will come to you.*
22. *Receive, please, instruction from His mouth, And lay up His words in your heart.*
24. *Then you will lay your gold in the dust, And the gold of Ophir among the stones of the brooks.*
Job 22:21,22 &24 NKJV

Flowing rivers of blessings and immeasurable treasures are stored in God. When you take God into your deepest parts and couple with Him in intense heart to heart communion, He releases Himself in you in His awesomeness. You become super-abundantly wealthy.

2. *My purpose is that they may be encouraged in heart and united in love, so that they may have the full riches of complete understanding, in*

*order that they may know the mystery of God,
namely, Christ,*

3. *In whom are hidden all the treasures of wisdom
    and knowledge.*

Colossians 2:2-3 NIV

We need to live in obedience to God and God's will. Obedience is the key. Intimacy with God is walking with God by His Word, in His faithful service, in prayer, worship and evangelism with a heart of pleasing God. All that we do in God and for God must be because we want to please Him. Intimacy is partaking of God's deepest nature, walking with Him in sincerity to share in His person.

You cannot walk with God intimately and remain downtrodden, frustrated, impoverished and unfulfilled! For instance, you cannot be an intimate friend of a wealthy nation's president and not be exposed to fame, riches and power. You would not even need to ask. The fact that you are close friends to 'Mr. President' will make men favour you.

How then can you be intimate with the God of the whole universe, the one who has the whole of creation in the palm of His hand, and still remain a nonentity?

* * *

When we do not know God and His ways, when we are not familiar with God and His purposes, we badger and pester

Him with requests and petitions of physical and material wealth and abundance. Sometimes against His desires for our lives and destinies but because of our importunity, He grants us our request of physical prosperity but we are starved of true riches.

> 13. *They soon forgot His works, they did not wait for His counsel.*
> 14. *But lusted exceedingly in the wilderness, and tested God in the desert.*
> 15. *And He gave them their request, but sent leanness into their soul.*
> Psalm 106: 13,14 & 15 NKJV

When we are focused on our needs and problems we are full of ourselves. When we lean on God completely, we can trust Him to work everything out right for us. When we get into God, we are full of God and invariably we are full of light and life.

When we are full of ourselves and our desires, we are full of death and darkness. When we do not seek God for who He is, our lives will be full of darkness and filth. When we do not desire a sincere close fellowship with God, but all we seek is our needs, concerns and wants, our lives will be full of rot and evil.

> 22. *The eye is the lamp of the body. So if your eye is sound, your entire body will be full of light.*

23. *But if your eye is unsound, your whole body will be full of darkness. If then the very light in you [your conscience] is darkened, how dense is that darkness!*

24. *No one can serve two masters; for either he will hate the one and love the other, or he will stand by and be devoted to the one and despise and be against the other. You cannot serve God and mammon (deceitful riches, money, possessions, or whatever is trusted in).*

25. *Therefore I tell you, stop being perpetually uneasy (anxious and worried) about your life, what you shall eat or what you shall drink; or about your body, what you shall put on. Is not life greater [in quality] than food, and the body [far above and more excellent] than clothing?*

Matthew 6:22-25

2. *The Lord looked down from heaven upon the children of men to see if there were any who understood, dealt wisely, and sought after God, inquiring for and of Him and requiring Him [of vital necessity].*

3. *They are all gone aside, they have all together become filthy; there is none that does good or right, no, not one*

Psalm 14:2-3

When we are eaten up with the desire to be rich, and affluent we will become dead inside, walking corpses, stinking, full of rottenness.

Outwardly then, there is affluence, glamour and seeming robustness, but inwardly there is lack, disease and death.

God desires that we prosper. God wants us to be happy and successful.

Beloved, I pray that you may prosper in every way and [that your body] may keep well, even as [I know] your soul keeps well and prospers.

3 John 2

The Lord shall open to you His good treasury, the heavens, to give the rain of your land in its season and to bless all the work of your hands; and you shall lend to many nations, but you shall not borrow.

Deuteronomy 28:12

God does not want us to live in frustration or in sadness. He does not want us to live unfulfilled and unfruitful lives. God wants us to live satisfied lives in Him.

16. You open Your hand and satisfy every living thing with favor.

Psalms 145:16 AMP

God wants us to have permanent wealth, not temporal riches. He desires for us everlasting prosperity. All these are locked up in deep communion with Him, serving Him and abiding in Him.

> *If they obey and serve Him, they shall spend their days in prosperity and their years in pleasantness and joy.*
>
> Job 36:11

Chapter Nineteen

MONEY DOES NOT DETERMINE YOUR VALUE

Value is the regard, the quality, the importance, the worth, the usefulness or the price of something or someone. Value indicates and reveals the kind of and the level of regard we have for something. Everything, every object, every entity has some level of value or worth attached to it.

One of the most accurate means to determine the value of something is by its price. The price paid for an object or an entity establishes its value. The price or cost of something or someone is a clear indication of the value and the worth of it. The price of an object or an entity is the total calculation of all the factors and resources involved in the production and manufacture of the object or entity. Everything that it takes to present a product as complete is the cost of that product. The cost or price of a product is the value of the product.

♦ **Money and value**

Money was created and introduced when trade by barter

became cumbersome, restricting and increasingly difficult to satisfy value for value, in the exchange of goods and services. Money was created to function as a more effective measure of value for goods and services.

Every product manufactured has a price. Every product costs something to put together. All the factors responsible to make a product ready for use are considered as the cost of production of that product. Everything that it takes to make a product complete is the cost of that product. The price or cost of the production or the manufacture of a product is the value of that product. When a product is purchased it has a price. The price is the value of the product expressed in terms of money.

Money was created to act as a measure of value for goods and services. Money expresses the value of material things. Money expresses the value of goods and services. Money functions as one of the best store of value, even though it is subject to fluctuations in value from time to time.

♦ Man and Money

Man's relationship with money started out with the aim of "ease of trade". Man used money as a portable, durable, acceptable and liquid medium of purchase for the things that he believed he needed but he could not produce on his own. He employed money to - store the value of, to exchange, and to account for, his goods.

Man's relationship with money started out as practical and remained so for as long as his needs were basic and functional. As man's needs moved from basic and functional to cosmetic, luxurious and ostentatious, his relationship with money became increasingly dysfunctional. The employee had gradually evolved to become the employer.

♦ **Jesus and Money**
Luke 16: 13-18

13 Imagine you're a servant and you have two masters giving you orders. What are you going to do when they have conflicting demands? You can't serve both, so you'll either hate the first and love the second, or you'll faithfully serve the first and despise the second. One master is God and the other is money. You can't serve them both. You can't work for God and work for money. 14 The Pharisees overheard all this, and they started mocking Jesus because they really loved money. Jesus (to the Pharisees): 15 You've made your choice. Your ambition is to look good in front of other people, not God. But God sees through to your hearts. He values things differently from the way you do. The goals you and your peers are reaching for God detests. 16 The law and the prophets had their role until the coming of John the Baptist. Since John's arrival, the good news of the kingdom of God has been taught while people are clamouring to enter it. 17 That's not to say that God's rules for living are useless. The stars in the sky and the earth beneath your feet will pass away before one letter of

God's rules for living become worthless.

♦ Man and Value

Every person wants to be seen as a person of great value and worth. Man has been trying forever to find and fix his value and worth on the highest level possible. Man has been using different scales and various standards of measure to evaluate himself so as to elevate himself in the eyes of the world to the loftiest heights ever.

♦ What is the price tag on Man?

Who or what determines the total calculation of all that it took to present the complete entity called man? Who can determine the worth of the creation that was made in the image and likeness of The Almighty God? What parameters or standards, would one use to evaluate the value of a human being, and how upright, how unbiased, how unprejudiced would such parameters be? What authority does anyone have to evaluate the worth of himself or of another?

The word 'authority' is derived from two words- 'author' and 'ity'. Author means- originator or creator. 'ity' is a suffix that simply indicates a 'state', (in this case), the state of being a creator. Author + ity = 'author'ity', meaning therefore, "the state of being a creator".

God Almighty is The Creator.

"So God created man in His own image, in the image of God created He him; male and female created He them." - Gen1:27.

GOD is the AUTHORITY on the life of man. He is the Creator and the Originator of man. He is the one who can adequately and successfully evaluate the value, the worth of man.

In God's word, Gen1:28 says you are made in the image and likeness of the greatest entity, God.

Gen1:31 states that God looked at everything He made and as high as His standards must be, He commented on how good His creation was, and that is talking about you.

Ecc3:11 says you are beautiful through and through, a finished product of originality and uniqueness; You cannot be undone.

Zech2:8 tells about you being the apple of God's eye, and Is43:4 clearly states that you are precious to Him, and honourable and He loves you with a passion.

You mean more to God than every resource, every gem put together in the whole world. You are the worthiest and the most valuable of all His creation. Even the angels in heaven are made lower than you- Ps 8. He calls you a King- Rev1:6.

You are so valuable to the Lord and Master of all creation that He paid a huge price for you. As far back as when you did not even exist on the earth, when you were nothing to yourself and a non entity to the whole world, He recognised you and placed a huge value on you; He gave up His Son to die for you,

He sacrificed His only son for you so as to establish and to preserve your value.

God put a price tag on you. The price tag on you is - The blood of Jesus, The Life of God. The price tag on Man is Jesus Christ. You were bought with a very high price.

1Peter 1:18&19 - (i)"knowing, as you do, that it was not with a ransom of perishable wealth, such as silver or gold, that you were set free from your frivolous habits of life which had been handed down to you from your forefathers, but with the precious blood of Christ—as of an unblemished and spotless lamb."

(ii)"You know that a price was paid to redeem you from following the empty ways handed on to you by your ancestors; it was not paid with things that perish (like silver and gold), but with the costly precious blood of the Anointed one - Jesus, that perfect and unblemished sacrificial lamb."

♦ **The Life of God – The Value of Man**

Your value is not based on material things that can perish. Your worth can never be determined by money, or houses, or garments, or any material acquisition or achievements. Money fails, houses burn down, garments wear out. The worth of a man can never be measured by things that can turn to nothing in an instant. Your value and worth in life is not determined by money or material things.

Luke 12:15-"And Jesus went on to say to them all, "Watch out and guard yourselves from every kind of greed; because a person's life is not about having a lot of possessions, no matter how rich you may be."

Man was not designed to be evaluated by money. Money does not possess the power nor the capacity to determine the value or worth of man.

Money and riches can never increase you as a person, it can increase your bank balance but not your person. Material wealth can never fill the void inside a person.

Ecclesiastes 5:10

(i)   *"If you love money, you will never be satisfied; if you long to be rich, you will never get all you want. It is useless."*

(ii)   *"Whoever loves money will never have enough money. Whoever loves luxury will not be content with abundance. This also is pointless."*

♦ Money is limited

Money acts as a measure of value for "things". Money is a measure of value for "goods". Money purchases goods and services. Money's capacity is limited, it can only purchase material things. Material things are coverings, they are drapes. They don't wash away filth, or pain, or shame, or dissatisfaction. Money cannot take away an inferiority complex nor can it remove feelings of extreme inadequacy. Money can only address the externals, it cannot repair or heal an afflicted or damaged soul. Abundance of money, affluence and riches can get a person expensive clothing, big houses, fancy cars, smooth skin and high seats in society, yet it will still be obvious to all that he is a complete non entity. Nabal was such a one.

"There was a certain man in Maon who carried on his business in the region of Carmel. He was very prosperous—three thousand sheep and a thousand goats, and it was sheep-shearing time in Carmel. The man's name was Nabal (Fool), a Calebite, and his wife's name was Abigail. The woman was intelligent and good-looking, the man brutish and mean". – 1 Samuel 25: 2&3

His riches could not make him a person of value. Money is not a measure of value for man.

Money cannot add value to a person, nor can it determine the worth of a person, only God can. God is the measure of value for man. The blood of Jesus is the measure of value for man. The Life of God is the measure of value for you. When God purchased man at an invaluable price, it revealed God's personal opinion regarding the value of what He purchased. By the price that God paid for you He openly established your worth – priceless. That purchase was the beginning of an awesome work of validation in you. The more you open up to accept all that Jesus has done in you and begin to see yourself as He sees you, the more your value manifests to you and to your world.

All that it takes to put a product together and make it complete is calculated to get the price of that product. You do not come cheap. It took the life of God to make you complete. That is some heavy price. When Jesus closed that deal, He exclaimed, "it is finished!" Nothing more to add. Money can not add to what the Life of God has completed. You do not need money or material things to validate what God has proclaimed as complete.

Money does not have the power nor the capacity to determine or define your value or your worth.

It is an attack on the integrity of the finished work of Christ for you or for anyone to evaluate your life or the life of another based on the amount of money or of material wealth the person possesses or does not possess. Luke 5:10-"Then he said, "Beware! Guard against every kind of greed. Life is not measured by how much you own."

We place too much emphasis on the material. We cut God out of the picture when we are so preoccupied with physical and material things. When we lose focus on God and who He is, we become confused about who we are and why we are here on earth. The emptiness created from loss of focus on God is usually quite deep. The emptiness brings a sense of deprivation, a lack of content and purpose. It is a gnawing void that creates a rabid passion for material supremacy and material glory. We centre our entire existence on acquisition of material wealth and it's attendant affluence, for we believe only then can our lives amount to much in the eyes of the world.

As humans our systems of value can at best only be partial, broken and hold to a subjective. Based on our – Background – Exposure   - Experience

The socio-economic difficulties of our background and our environment should not permeate our psyche to the extent that it blocks us out of the truth of God.

Jesus spoke to the Pharisees regarding their love of money and their insatiable hunger for material wealth. He told them plainly that His measure of value was different from theirs. We place value on things which serve our purposes or give us pleasure, but to agree with God is to value that which serves God's purposes and gives God pleasure. It brings us into a completely different system of determining value.

In Conclusion - Your value and worth is in the truth of God. The standard of determining value belongs to God. God alone sees the complete picture from the beginning to the end. He knows the times and seasons of all men, how we all start off and how we end. He alone can determine the accurate and absolute worth of an entity. When we agree with God's standards and measures, we leave the temporal, myopic and biased realm and enter into the supernatural, the accurate and the full picture.

You are worth much more than all the money, all the riches, all the wealth in creation. Your value is God.

"For God so dearly loved and prized us all that He gave His only Son so that all who believe in Him will not be lost, they will not be destroyed, they will not be insignificant, nor inconsequential, but they will become whole and have meaningful, boundless and everlasting life."

— John 3:16

Chapter Twenty

FLOWING IN LOVE

We receive salvation as a gift of Love. We come to the saving grace of Christ Jesus by love. We are called to love. God is all about love.

> 29. *Jesus answered, The first and principal one of all commands is: Hear, O Israel, The Lord our God is one Lord.*
>
> 30. *And you shall love the Lord your God out of and with your whole heart and out of and with all your soul (your life) and out of and with all your mind (with your faculty of thought and your moral understanding) and out of and with all your strength. This is the first and principal commandment.*
>
> 31. *The second is like it and is this, You shall love your neighbor as yourself. There is no other commandment greater than these.*
> Mark 12:29-31 (Emphasis Added)

When we truly live in love, we live in God and God lives in us. We cannot abide in God without love. When we have the love of God in us, we will seek God more. The more we love God, the more of God we know. Love is a heart and life thing. When you love, you get your heart and your whole life involved. When we love God, we are involved with Him with our spirit, soul and body. We want to give Him our all. We want to know Him deeply. We devour His word because we want to feel His heartbeat, we want to know His mind. We pray because we want to wrap ourselves in His ever comforting, reassuring strength and presence.

> And so we know and rely on the love God has for us.
>
> 1 John 4:16 NIV

When we are in a love relationship with God, our whole being is saturated with God. The more we get involved with God in love, the less we are concerned about amassing earthly riches.

15. *Do not love or cherish the world or the things that are in the world. If anyone loves the world, love for the Father is not in him.*

16. *For all things is in the world - the lust of the flesh [craving for sensual gratification] and the lust of the eyes [greedy longings of the mind] and the pride of life [assurance in one's own resources or in the stability of earthly things] - these do not come from the Father but are from the world [itself].*

17. And the world passes away and disappears, and with it the forbidden cravings (the passionate desires, the lust) of it; but he who does the will of God and carries out His purposes in his life abides (remains) forever

1 John 2:15-17

The Laodicean church, the prosperous church, the church whose main preoccupation was earthly blessings, wealth, riches, affluence, fame, etc; this worldly church had all earthly provisions but God called them "wretched, miserable, poor, blind and naked."

For you say, I am rich; I have prospered and grown wealthy, and I am in need of nothing; and you do not realize and understand that you are wretched, pitiable, poor, blind, and naked.

Revelations 3:17

Earthly possessions, physical and material prosperity are not the same as joy, peace and fulfillment. Apostle Paul enjoined the worldly church to take up love and walk in it. He exposed to them the true riches and true wealth hidden in the knowledge of Christ Jesus.

1. *I want you to know that I am trying very hard to help you. And I am trying to help the people in Laodicea and other people who have never seen me.*

2. *I want them to be strengthened and joined together with love. I want them to have the full confidence that comes from understanding. I mean I want them to know fully the secret truth that God has made known. That truth is Christ himself.*

3. *In Christ all the treasures of wisdom and knowledge are safely kept.*

4. *I tell you these things so that no person can fool you by telling you ideas that seem good, but are false.*

Colossian 2:1-4 ETRV

Paul further admonished them not to follow those who deceive them by teaching that they seek Christ Jesus because they want to prosper materially, physically and financially. Rather, they should seek Christ because of His nature and because of who He is.

For in Christ we are full and in need of nothing else.

And in Christ you are full. You need nothing else.
Christ is ruler over all rulers and powers.

Colossians 2:10 ETRV

God works in man from the inside to the outside. God begins His work from within man's spirit and then shines His light from there on to the outside.

God designed man originally for fellowship. God wants us to commune with Him. He wants us to walk with Him.

8. *And they heard the sound of the Lord God*
   walking in the garden in the cool of the day,
   and Adam and his wife hid themselves from
   the presence of the Lord God among the
   trees of the garden.
9. *But the Lord God called to Adam and said*
   to him, Where are you?

Genesis 3:8-9

We cannot see God physically, nor can we relate to Him with our physical selves. We can only relate to God with our spirits. Our spirit was designed to relate to God and then transmit this relationship into our soul and then our body.

The fellowship we have with Him in the spirit will manifest in our soul and our body, thereby flooding and filling our entire being with the essence of God. God will be obvious to people in the way we walk and in the way we behave.

God desires for us to relate with Him earnestly and sincerely. He wants us to seek Him for who He is, not only for what He can give or what He can do.

> 23. *A time will come, however, indeed it is already here, when the true (genuine) worshipers will worship the Father in spirit and in truth (reality); for the Father is seeking just such people as these as His worshipers.*
>
> 24. *God is a Spirit (a spiritual Being) and those who worship Him must worship Him in spirit and in truth (reality).*
>
> John 4:23-24

God wants a deep, heart to heart, one-on-one fellowship with us. He wants to touch us from deep within us. God wants us to receive Him into our lives with singleness of heart and purpose in true love. WHATEVER WE DESIRE CAN ONLY BE ACHIEVED WHEN WE WILLINGLY, SINCERELY, WHOLE-HEARTEDLY RECEIVE HIM FOR WHO HE IS.

> *Then they were quite willing and glad for Him to come into the boat. And now the boat went at once to the land they had steered toward. [And <u>immediately</u> they reached the shore toward*

which they had been slowly making their way.]
John 6:21 (Emphasis added)

We were created by God for Himself not for ourselves. God created us for Himself, for His purposes, for His plans. God created us for His own pleasure, not for our own pleasures. God created us to satisfy Himself, not to satisfy ourselves.

> *Worthy are You, our Lord and God, to receive the glory and the honor and dominion, for You created all things; by Your will they were [brought into being] and were created.*
>
> Revelations 4:11

We have all sinned and come short of God's perfection. Our righteousness, our best and purest without His grace is nothing but pure filth. No one can stand before Him and claim to be clean.

All the same God desires to do a work of goodness and perfection in us. He wants us to sincerely open ourselves up to Him so that He by Himself might work a good work in us. Only God can make us pure and righteous, and He will start that work from our inner selves.

When God relates with us in our inner selves, we are transformed from the inside to the outside, then we manifest the life and light of God in our outward life. The light and glory of God on the inside of us is transmitted from the inside and begins to reflect in everything we think, we do (in secret and in the open) and we say (our language, our speech). We begin to live godly lives from inside and then to the outside.

He wants to touch our lips, our hearts, our hands, our feet. So our hearts flow with pure thoughts, our lips speak clean, peaceable words, our hands do right things and our feet walk in godliness. He wants to transform our whole being. God wants to do a complete work in us.

As we carry God on our insides, He is transmitted from the inside unto the outside. People all around us see God in us. They see God in everything that comes out of us, in everything that concerns us.

When we carry God on our insides, we carry His power, His awesomeness; so we become untouchable by life's circumstances and situations. We are in the world, but not of the world. The conditions of life have no adverse negative effects on us. The life we live is bursting forth straight from the inexhaustible, ever flowing fountain of the life of God.

God Himself then achieves His plans and purposes in us. He takes us to His desired height for us in life and in ministry. God designs for us, He supports us and He identifies with us in all that we do.

As we flow with Him in true, sincere, ceaseless communion, He will reveal to us and in us the magnitude of His wealth, riches, wisdom and knowledge.

Oh, the depth of the riches both of the wisdom and knowledge of God! How unsearchable are His judgments and His ways past finding out!
                                        Romans 11:33 NKJV

As we cooperate with His plan and purpose for our lives, He will manifest Himself in our lives and ministry in awesome ways that are beyond human comprehension and working. He will manifest in us beyond what we desire, what we ask or what could have entered our minds concerning our lives.

Now to him Who, by (in consequence of) the [action of His] power that is at work within us, is able to [carry out His purpose and] do superabundantly, far over and above all that we [dare] ask or think [infinitely beyond our highest prayers, desires, thoughts, hopes, or dreams]
                                        Ephesians 3:20

We ought to allow God to start working in us from within. Whatever God desires for us, He will start working it in us from within first and then bring it to manifestation on the outside.

When we open our inner selves to God, He will come in into our innermost and fill us with Himself.

Behold, I stand at the door and knock; if anyone hears and listens to and heeds My voice and opens the door, I will come in to him and will eat with him, and he [will eat] with Me.

Revelations 3:20

God wants to project Himself through us. He wants our lives to be showpieces for Him. God wants His beauty and glory to manifest in our day-to-day life. He wants us to speak His words, sing His songs and fill the whole earth with His melody.

God desires to have a love relationship with us in our inward parts. He desires for us to open up our hearts for Him. God wants to fill us with His light in this dark world. God wants to shine in us, through us and by us light up the entire universe. Then, will we truly fulfill our calling in life as light so that the world may be a better place because we are in it.

In Matthew 5:14, God calls us Christians '… the light of the world.' It means the world is in need of illumination because darkness exists there. God is saying our function is light. That means there is darkness for us to illuminate.

Isaiah 60:1 says, "Arise, Shine…" Verse 2 of the same chapter of Isaiah reads, "for behold the darkness shall cover the earth, gross darkness the people, BUT He, the Lord, shall arise upon you…"

We must make a conscious concerted effort to SHINE so that darkness can be dispelled. "Arise" and "Shine" are two seriously active words. We must stand up to our responsibility. We must mount up, tower above, to give light, to show light, to set on fire for God.

As light, we have the singular calling to function as illuminator. We must change the situation of our environment for good. We must affect out surroundings positively.

Light makes visibility better. People see clearer and better for light. Light brings edification, elucidation, and instruction. When we function as light we dispel confusion. Our lives give instruction to right living. Our speech, out attitude, our manner edifies and improves.

When we function as light, it means we ourselves are filled with light. Jesus Christ is the true light that lights every man.

> *There it was - the true Light [was then] coming into the world [the genuine, perfect, steadfast Light] that illumines every person.*
>
> John 1:9

When we associate and relate in intimacy with Him, we ourselves become illuminated by His great light. The more we associate with Him, the more light we appropriate.

If we say we are children of God and there is no light in us, for the light that should be in us is darkness, then we have failed in our calling as light.

35. See to it, then, that the light within you is not darkness.

36. Therefore, if your whole body is full of light, and no part of it dark, it will be completely lighted, as when the light of a lamp shines on you."

Luke 11:35 & 36 NIV

When we say we are born again believers but instead of dispelling darkness, we ourselves are the authors of darkness, then our lives have no meaning, it is a waste.

Our attitudes, our life styles, are supposed to edify and bring people closer to God. Our speech, our character is supposed to make people love God not despise Him.

Light is not anger, profanities and vulgarities; these are darkness. We should not defile and contaminate the environment with our speech and attitude. Anger is a pollutant. Selfishness, stubbornness, rudeness, immorality, insulting and abusive words are pollutants - they bring darkness around us.

When we refuse to exhibit the goodness, the love, the kindness, the compassion of the gospel to our environment, we are failures as light.

People must acknowledge that we are light.

Let your light so shine before men, that they may see your good works, and glorify your Father which is in heaven.

Matthew 5:16 KJV (Emphasis added)

If we are indeed light, we will shine. Light has no other function than to illuminate, to shine. Light that cannot illuminate or shine has lost its function and is fit only to be castaway.

We have been called light. This means that we have the ability and capacity to shine. We must take up our mandate and begin to fulfill it.

The more we associate, rub minds and commune with Jesus Christ, The Light of the World, the more we ourselves are filled with light. Our lives and situation then begin to manifest light. We now function as light wherever we are. All who hear us, see us, speak with us and interact with us will acknowledge that we are glowing and shining in God's goodness and excellence. This is prosperity.

Let your light so shine before men that they may see your moral excellence and your praiseworthy, noble, and good deeds and recognize and honor and praise and glorify your Father Who is in heaven.

Matthew 5:16

Chapter Twenty-One

BEAUTY WITHIN AND WITHOUT

Outward beauty that does not come from within is deceptive and unreliable. Outward presentations of beauty that do not flow from the inner man, have no depth, no root. This kind of beauty fades and withers.

Beauty is excellence. Excellence that stems from within a man flows automatically to the outward life of that man.

Beauty by the world's standards is physical; that is, what the eye can see. The world's definition of beauty concentrates on and emphasizes physical manifestations. This beauty is all about form and feature.

The world's standard of beauty is self-indulgent, it promotes self, it luxuriates self. This standard of beauty promotes feelings of insecurities and self-consciousness. It attacks self-confidence. It generates self-indulgent cravings. This standard of beauty makes you want to satisfy self, to promote the flesh.

Outward presentations of beauty that have no depth are only wrappings. The way you dress, the way you look, the cars you drive, the houses you own, the money and position you have acquired and attained, are all accessories. They are not the "real thing." All these are transient and temporal. These are externals.

The real substance is inside. True Beauty is from within. Everything starts from within. Creation started from within. All things grow from within to the outside. God gives life to all things from within.

Beauty is from inside. Beauty generates from integrity of heart and from strength of character. True beauty generates from virtues that are built from deep within the inner man, the inner self. True Beauty flows from inner cleanliness and purity.

True beauty shines, it glows, it is attractive to the mind, to the senses - and to the spirit. This beauty is irresistible and alluring. This beauty radiates and it over-shadows all physical inadequacies, shortcomings and blemishes.

True beauty is about what comes out from the inner man, how we think, how we talk, how we relate to people, the way we behave. This beauty is portrayed in how we affect people and situations.

Beauty enhances. Beauty is refreshing. Do we affect lives and situations this way? Do we enhance lives and situations? Does our manner, our attitude, bring refreshing?

The emphasis should not be on the outward man, it should be on the inward man, the inner man.

> 3. *Let not yours be the (merely) external adorning with (elaborate) interweaving and knotting of the hair, the wearing of jewelry, or changes of clothes;*
> 4. *But let it be the inward adorning and beauty of the hidden person of the heart, with the incorruptible and unfading charm of a gentle and peaceful spirit, which (is not anxious or wrought up, but) is very precious in the sight of God.*
>
> 1 Peter 3:3-4

The emphasis should not be on decorating or building the wrapper, the covering, the container. The emphasis should be on building the inner man, the character.

A person is ugly or beautiful because of the things that come out, emanate, flow out, from that person. A person is not ugly because of physical appearances or physical features or physical acquisition.

There is no ugly physical feature. There is only an ugly heart, an ugly inside. A person, out of the ugliness that is deposited deep within him exudes ugliness.

> 10. *On the seventh day, when the king's heart was merry with wine, he commanded Mehuman, Biztha, Harbona, Bigtha, Abagtha, Zethar, and Carkas, the seven*

eunuchs who ministered to King Ahasuerus as attendants,

11. *To bring Queen Vashti before the king, with her royal crown, to show the peoples and the princes her beauty, for she was fair to behold.*

12. *But Queen Vashti refused to come at the king's command conveyed by the eunuchs. Therefore the king was enraged, and his anger burned within him.*

Esther 1:10-12

Queen Vashti was beautiful on the outside, but she had ugliness deposited within her. She had pride, vanity and haughtiness inside her. This is an ugly person.

Beauty is from God. God is a God of beauty.

One thing have I asked of the Lord, that will I seek, inquire for, and [insistently] require: that I may dwell in the house of the Lord [in His presence] all the days of my life, to behold and gaze upon the beauty [the sweet attractiveness and the delightful loveliness] of the Lord and to meditate, consider, and inquire in His temple.

Psalms 27:4

We can see God's beauty displayed in the whole of creation. God's nature is beauty. He is beautiful in holiness.

> *Give to the Lord the glory due to His name; worship the Lord in the beauty of holiness or in holy array.*
>
> Psalms 29:2

God is perfect in beauty.

> *Out of Zion, the perfection of beauty, God shines forth.*
>
> Psalms 50:2

God wants us to be beautiful within and without. God wants us to be thoroughly, sincerely beautiful. God desires that beauty springs forth from deep within us and out to our outward man and our outward life.

God wants us to share His Nature of beauty. God wants us to partake in His beauty. God does not want us to have superficial beauty that is only on the surface, but has no substance, no depth.

God does not want us to have temporal beauty that will not last, that will fade and crumple easily. God desires us to be beautiful - spirit, soul and body.

God wants to flow from within us to our outward man, to our world, in true unadulterated undefiled beauty.

We should not be beautiful to behold only on the outside but full of worms and maggots on the inside. We should not be decorated graves. We should be beautiful through and through with no ugliness or defilements.

The Bible calls us priests.

> *But you are a chosen race, a royal priesthood, a dedicated nation, (God's) own purchased, special people, that you may set forth the wonderful deeds and display the virtues and perfections of Him who called you out of darkness into His marvelous light.*
>
> I Peter 2:9

> 5. *Now therefore, if you will obey My voice in truth and keep My covenant, then you shall be My own peculiar possession and treasure from among and above all peoples; for all the earth is Mine.*
> 6. *And you shall be to Me a kingdom of priests, a holy nation (consecrated, set apart to the worship of God). These are the words you shall speak to the Israelites.*
>
> Exodus 19:5-6

Every born-again believer is a priest of God. Every priest of God has a code of conduct: we must show forth God's beauty.

> 2. *And you shall make holy garments for Aaron your brother, for glory and for beauty.*
> 3. *So you shall speak to all who are gifted artisans, whom I have filled with the spirit of wisdom, that they may make Aaron's garments, to consecrate him, that he may minister to Me as priest.*
>
>   Exodus 28: 2-3 NKJV

As children of God, as priests of God we can only minister to God or serve God when we manifest His glory and His beauty. As children of God, as priests of God, we can only manifest God's beauty when we have His beauty deposited in our inner man, that is, in our character, our day-to-day attitudes. Our character shows who we are. Our character is our garment.

Attaining true lasting beauty is by close interaction with God who is "Beauty Personified." We can attain beauty, true beauty, by teaming up and associating closely with the Beautiful One - God.

As we associate intimately with Him in our inner man; in deep worship, in prayer, in reading and studying of His word and in sincere service to Him - we will begin to partake of His undefiled beauty from deep within us.

This beauty will penetrate into every area of our lives, our health, our home, our ministry, our finances, our children, our possessions, our career, our relationships, everything that concerns us.

As we continue to walk with Him in sincerity of heart and purpose, He will flow out to our outward life and beautify our physical life and world for all to see.

> *And let the beauty of the LORD our God be upon us: and establish thou the work of our hands upon us; yea, the work of our hands establish thou it.*
>
> Psalms 90:17 KJV

God's beauty flowing out of us will draw people to us and make us irresistible. We will stand out for good wherever we are or whatever we do.

God's beauty flowing from our lives will make room for us where there seems to be no room; and we will radiate God in all that comes out of us.

Physical acquisitions and accomplishments are outward effects. Material wealth, power, physical success, religious power, pomp and pageantry are all wrappings, mere envelopes.

Beauty is not meant to be just a covering. Beauty is not meant to be just a wrapping. Beauty is meant to be from within to without; this is when it is truly BEAUTY.

Open up yourself to God today and make your life, your world a truly beautiful place.

Please let us pray -
Almighty God, I acknowledge that you are God over all creation. I acknowledge the Holy Trinity of God The Father, God The Son; Jesus Christ, and God The Holy Spirit. Lord God, I desire a friendship relationship with you, I would like to be intimate with you. Jesus, please come and take over the affairs of my life and help me. Holy Spirit, hold me close and teach me to please you at all times. Cause my life to be an expression of your love, your life, your power. Let all who come in contact with me experience you. And at the close of ages, dear Lord, find me faithful and true. Thank you Jesus. In Jesus name I pray.
Amen.

.

Magda King is a pseudonym.

Kemi Jorge-Oyewusi had always wanted to write under the name Magda King. She was baptised into Christ and given the name Magdaline.

Kemi Jorge-Oyewusi is a prolific writer and she has authored a number of books - including children's books

inside back page

Printed in Great Britain
by Amazon